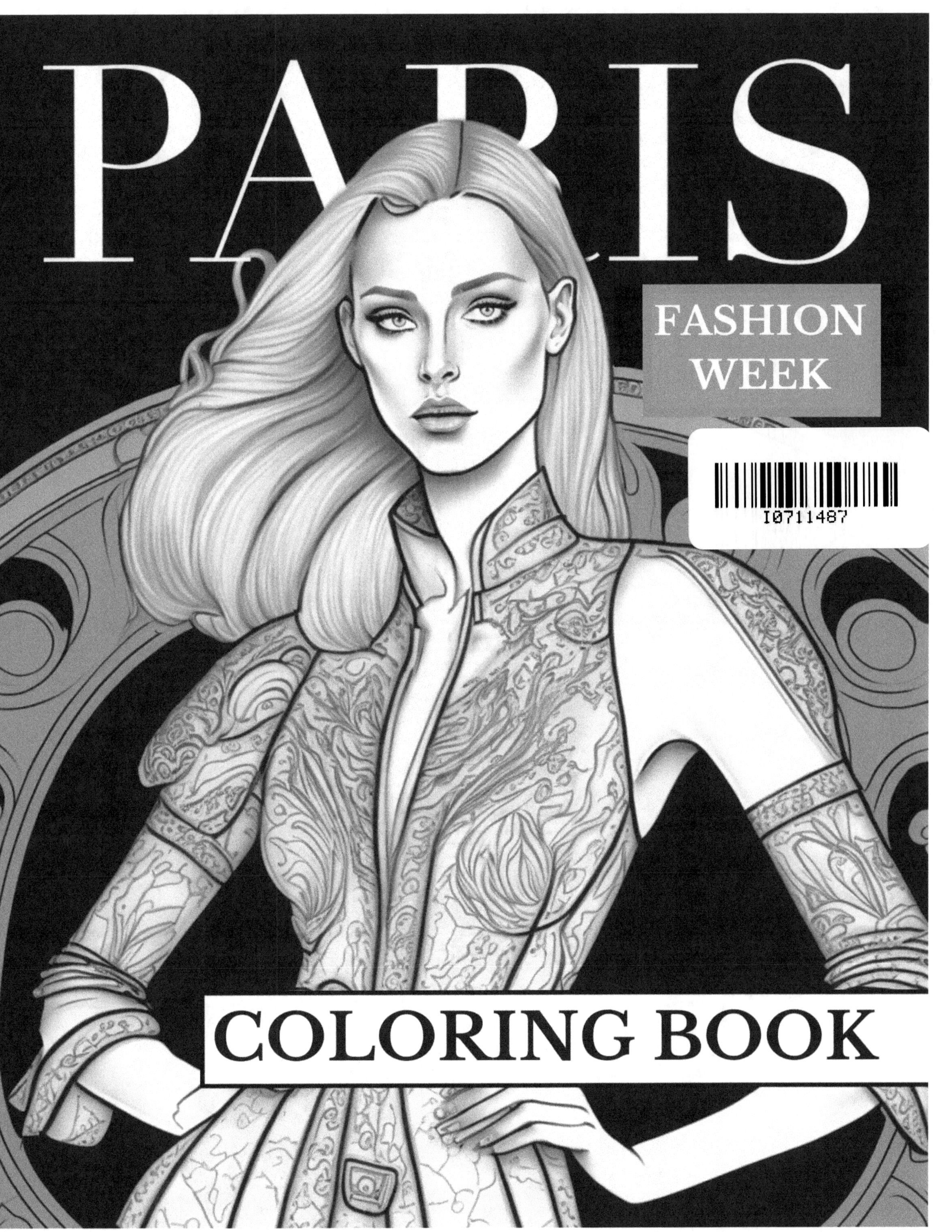

PARIS
FASHION WEEK
COLORING BOOK
I0711487

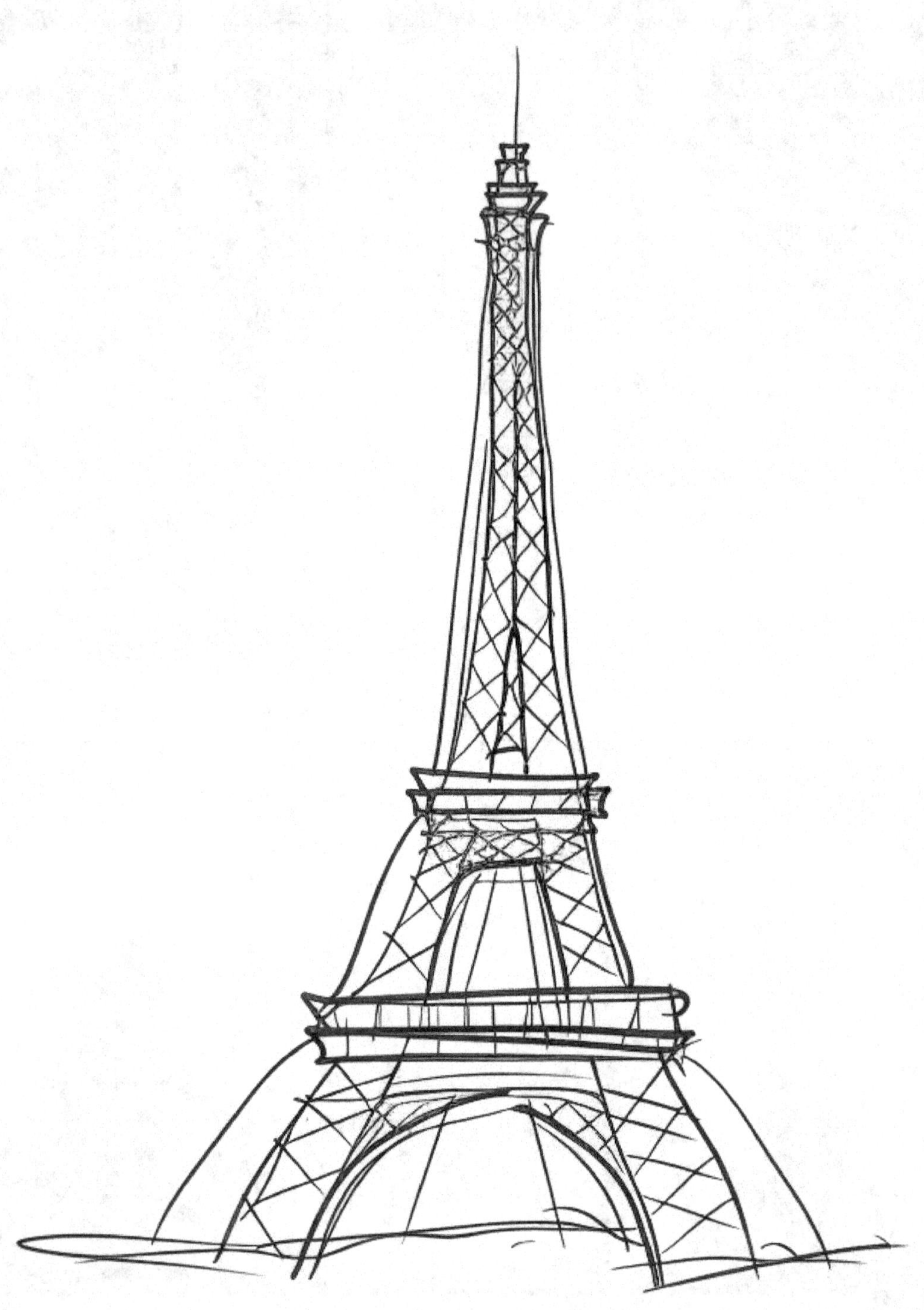

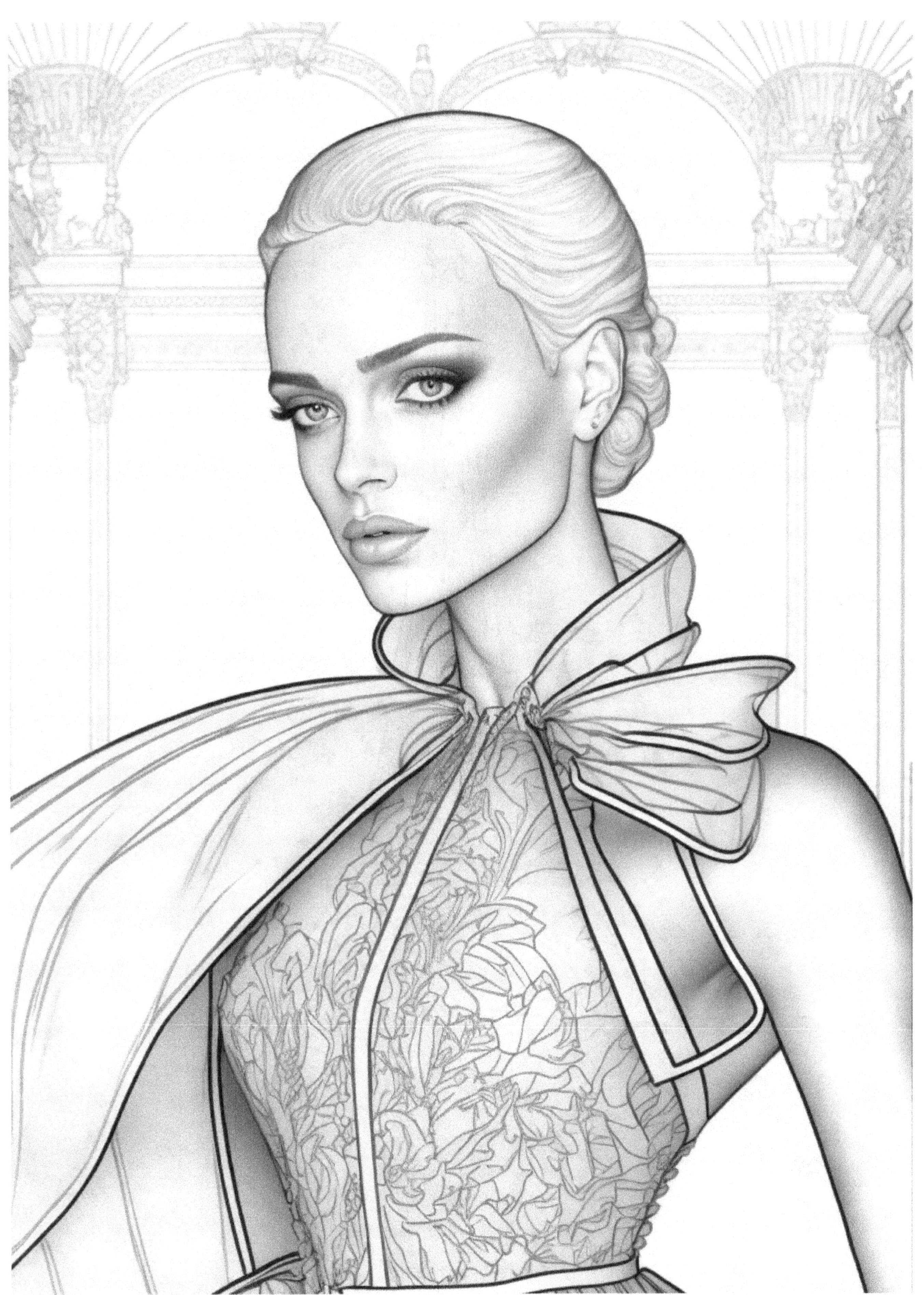

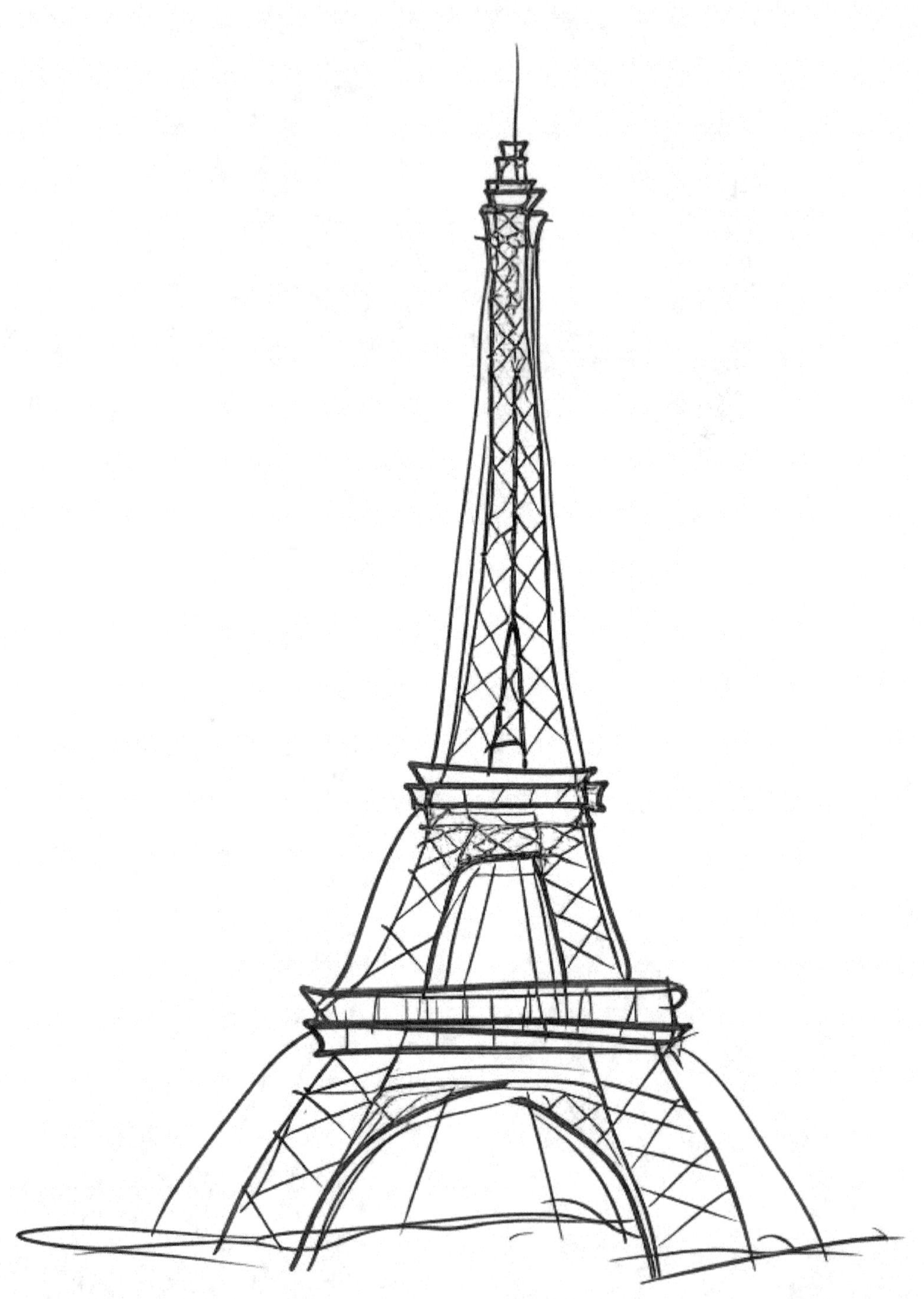

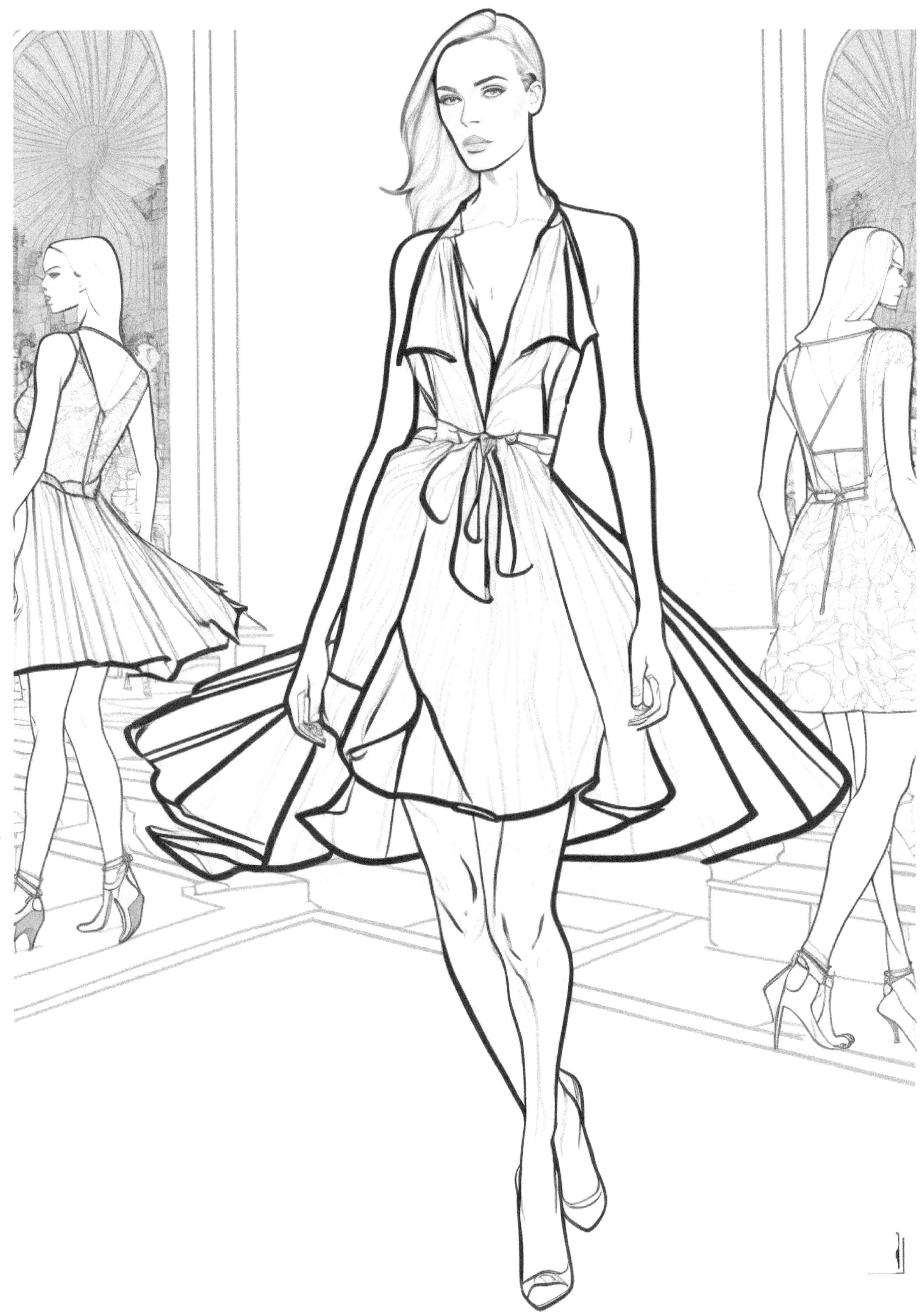

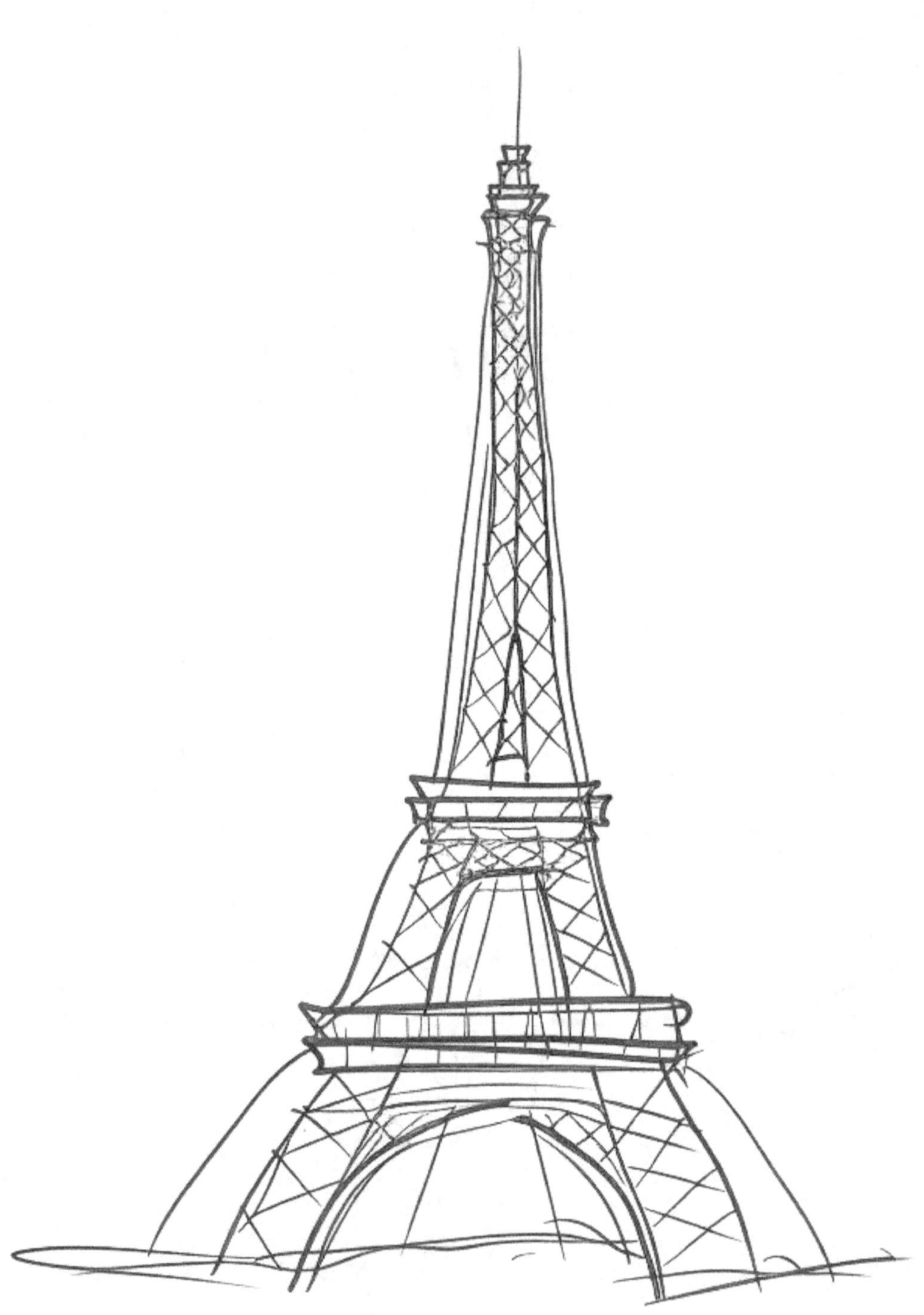

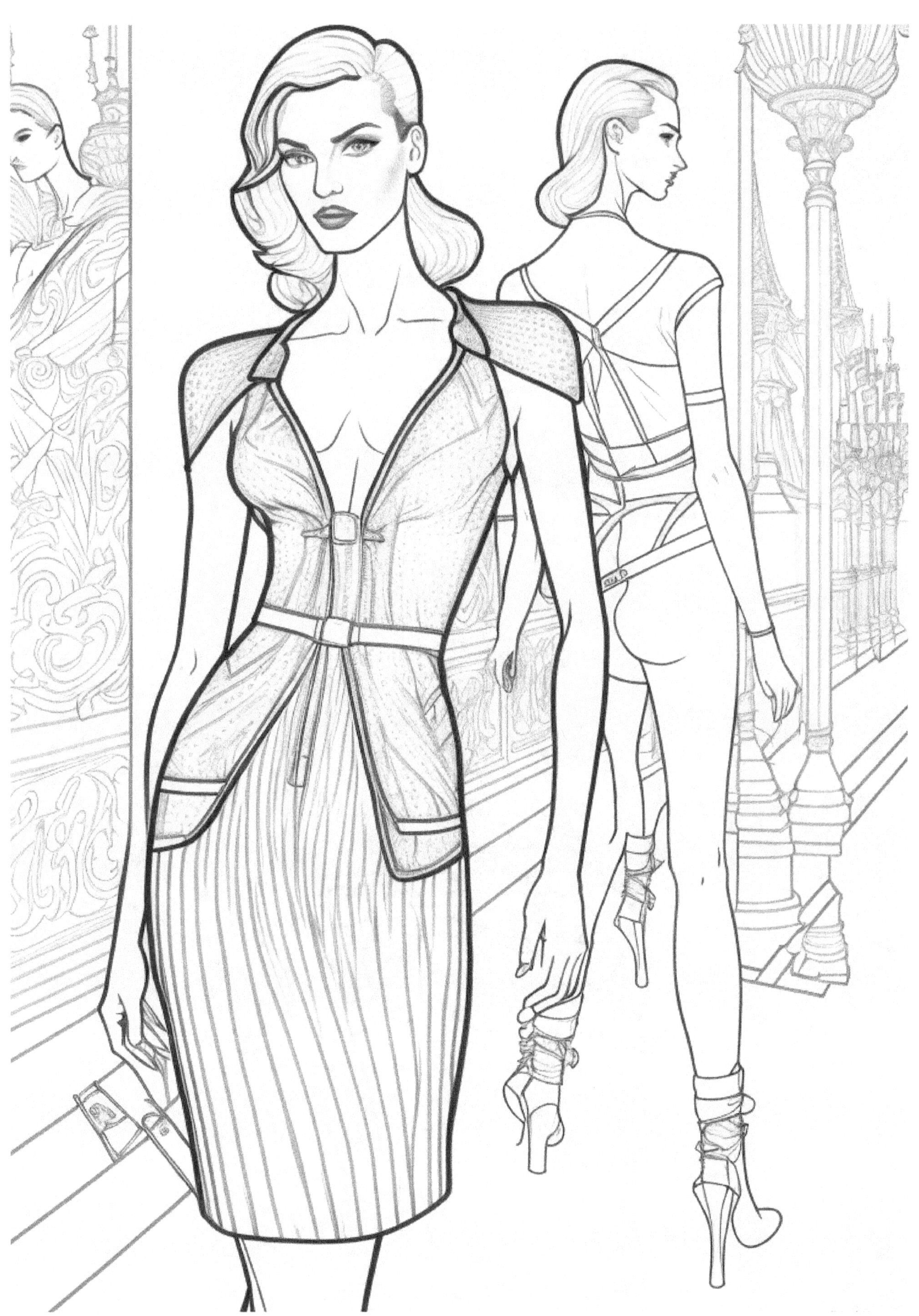

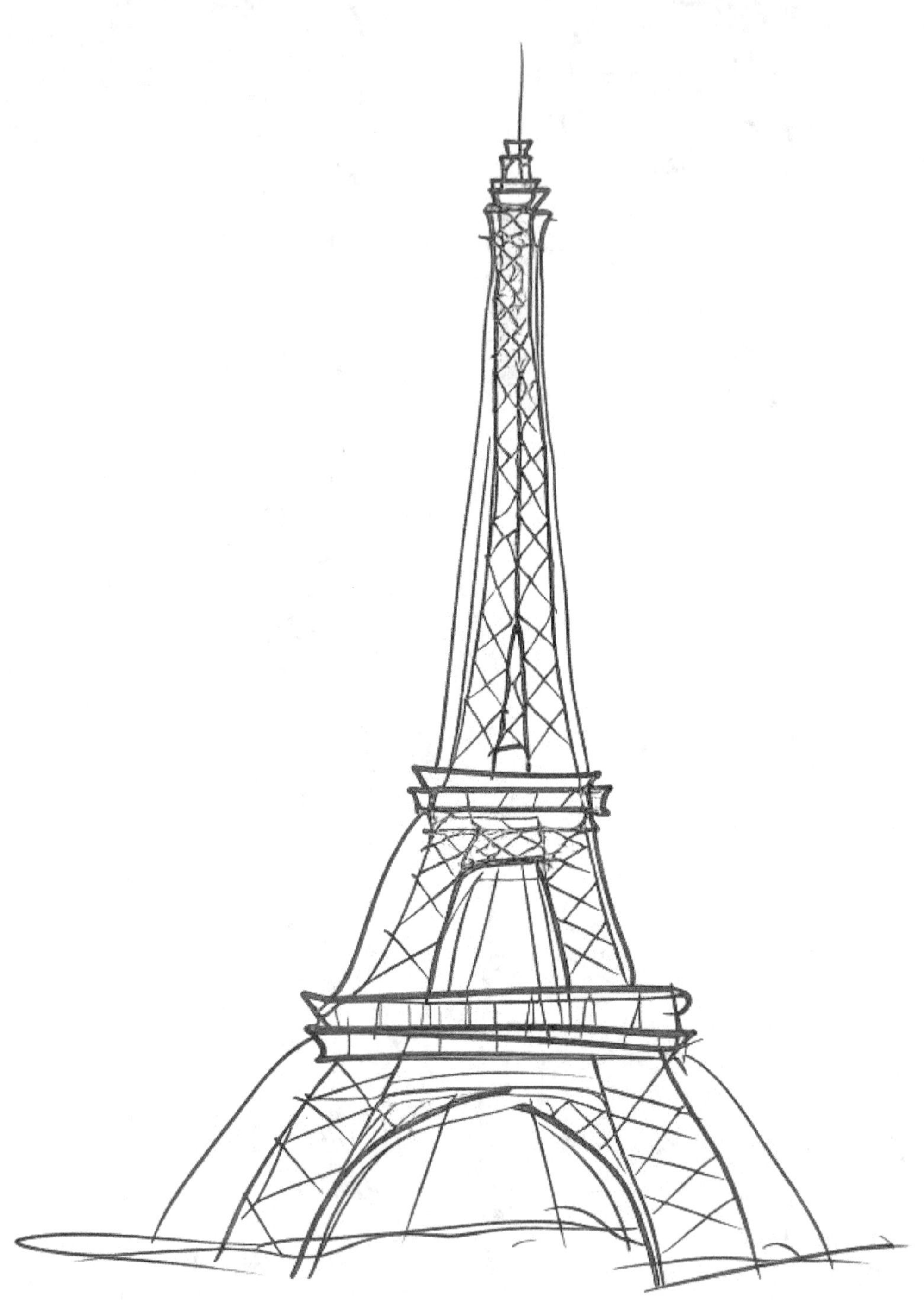

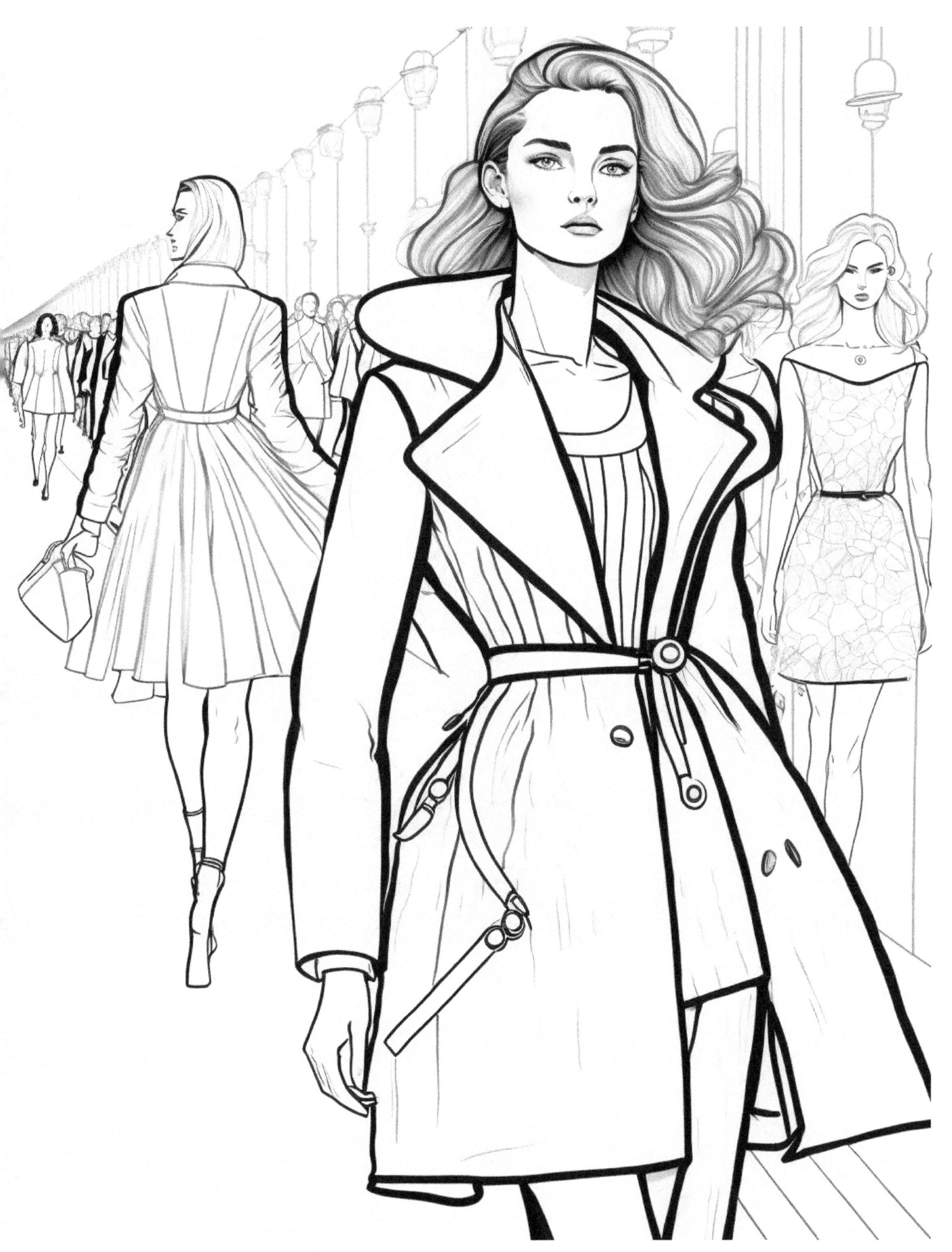

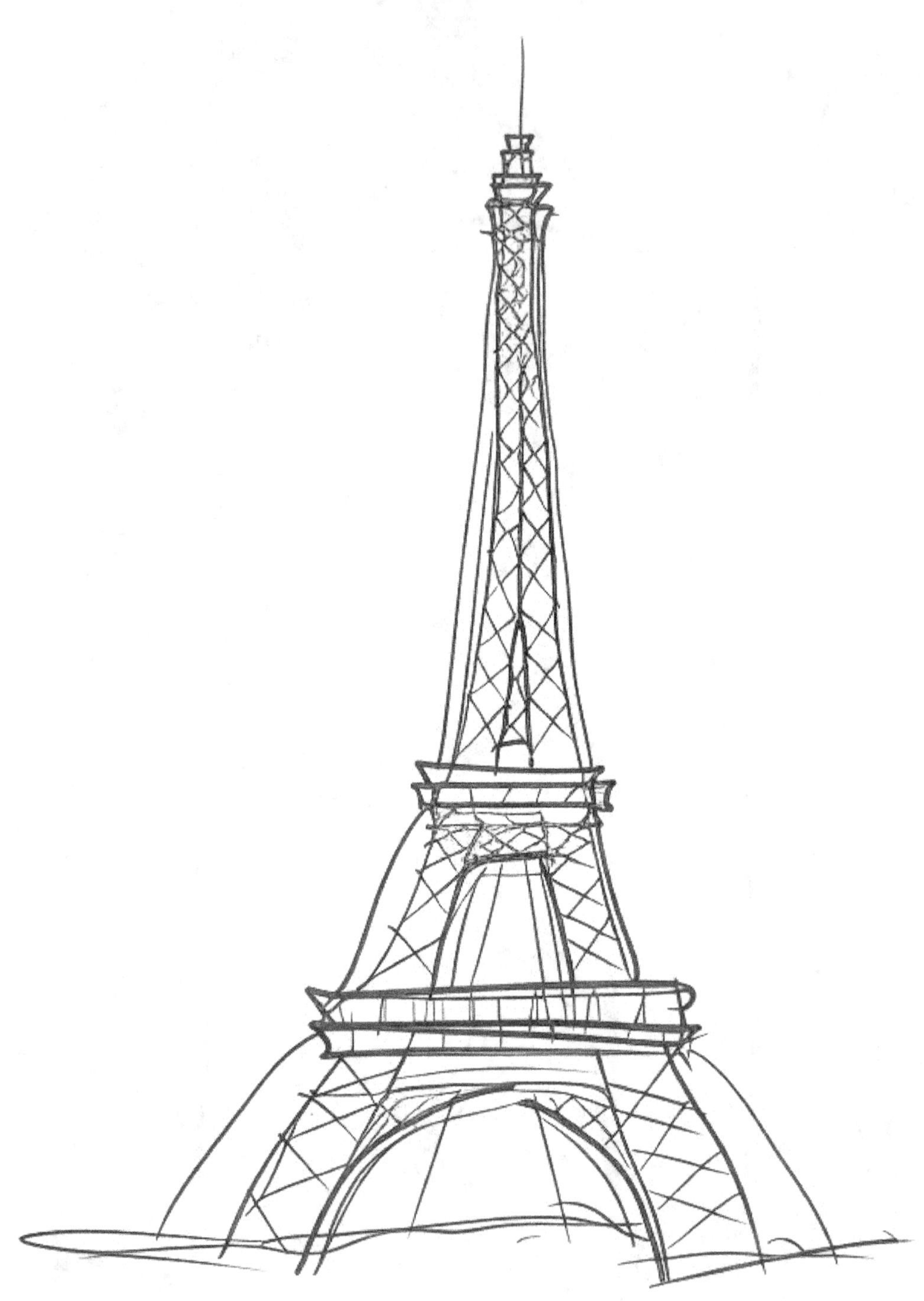

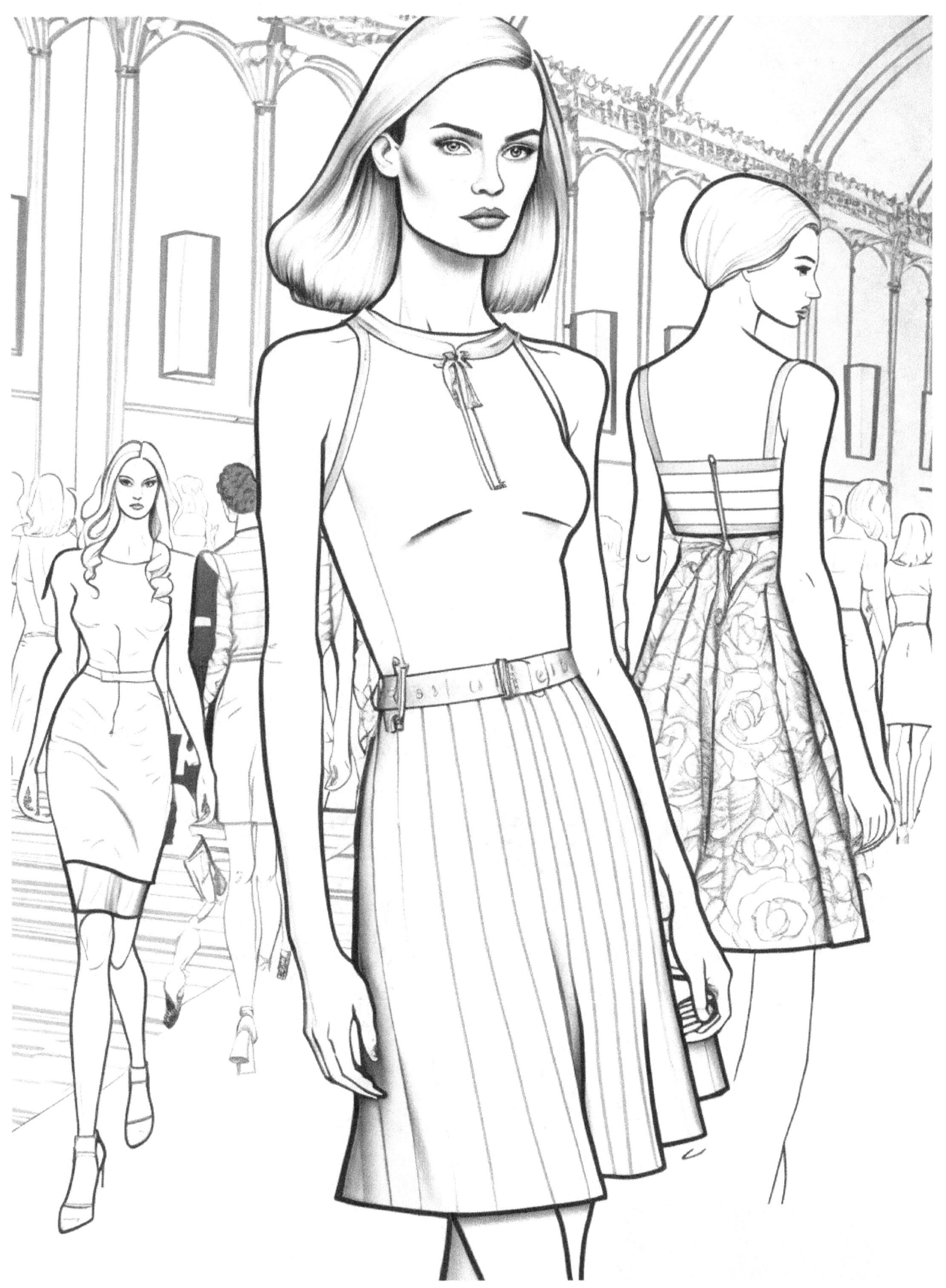

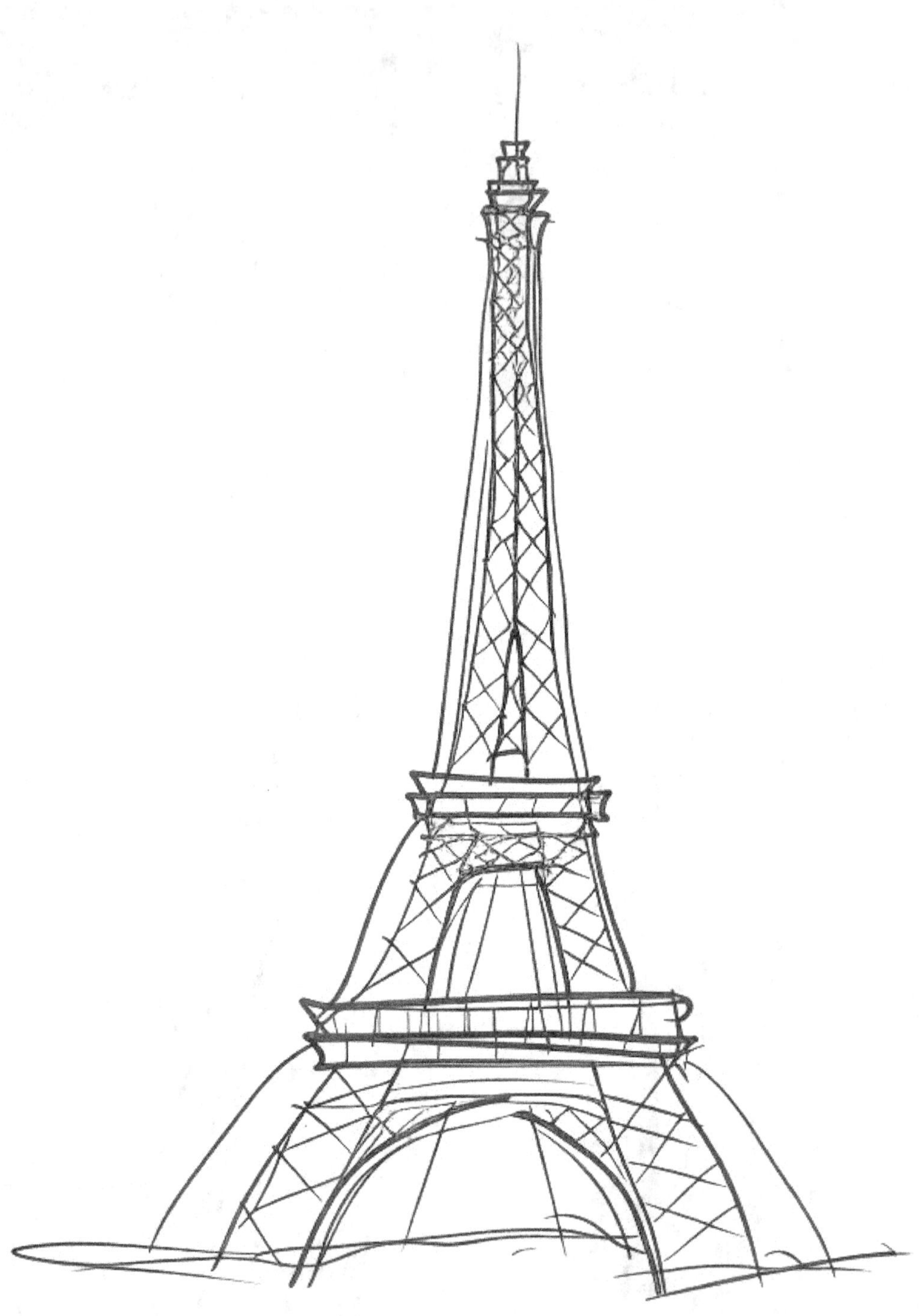

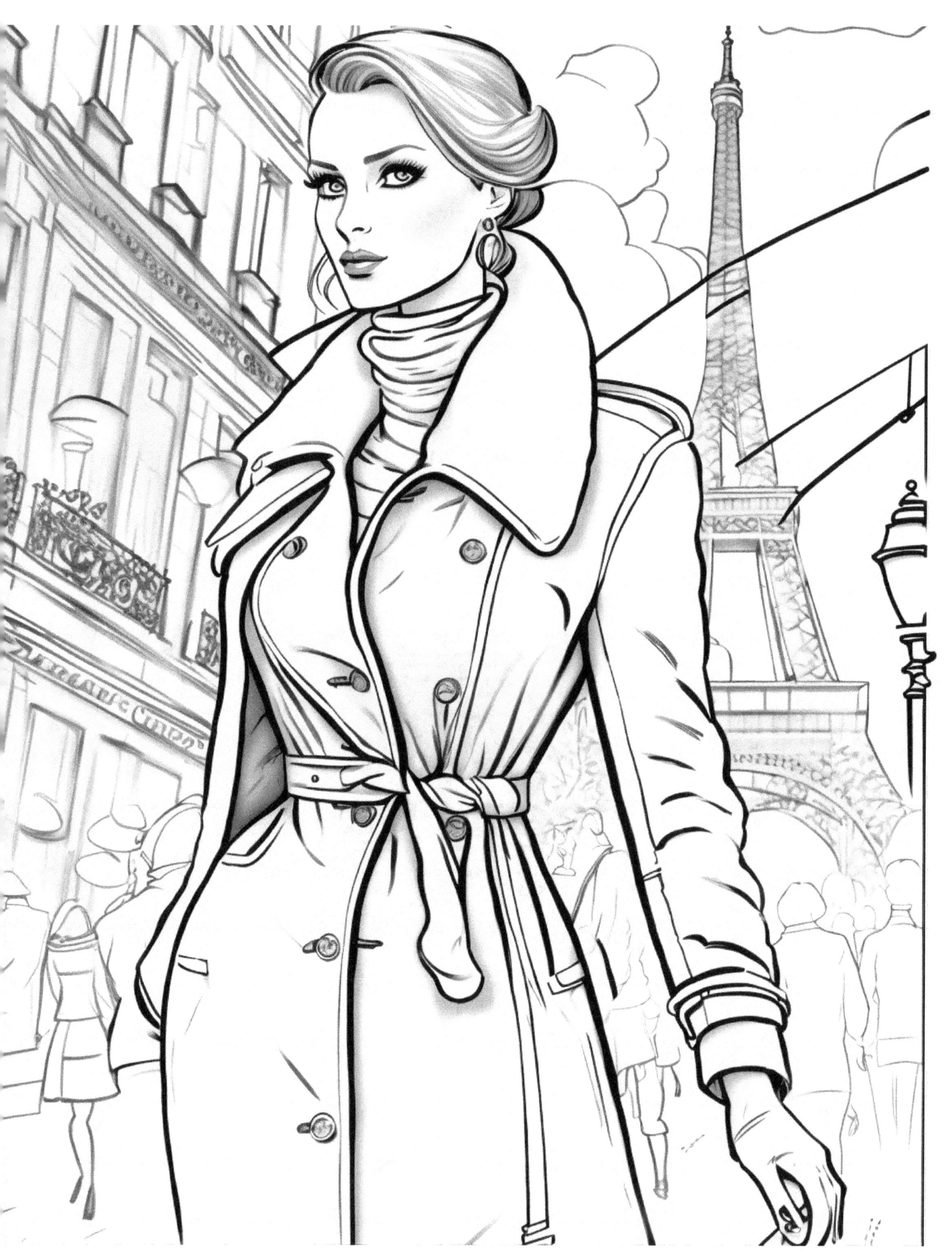

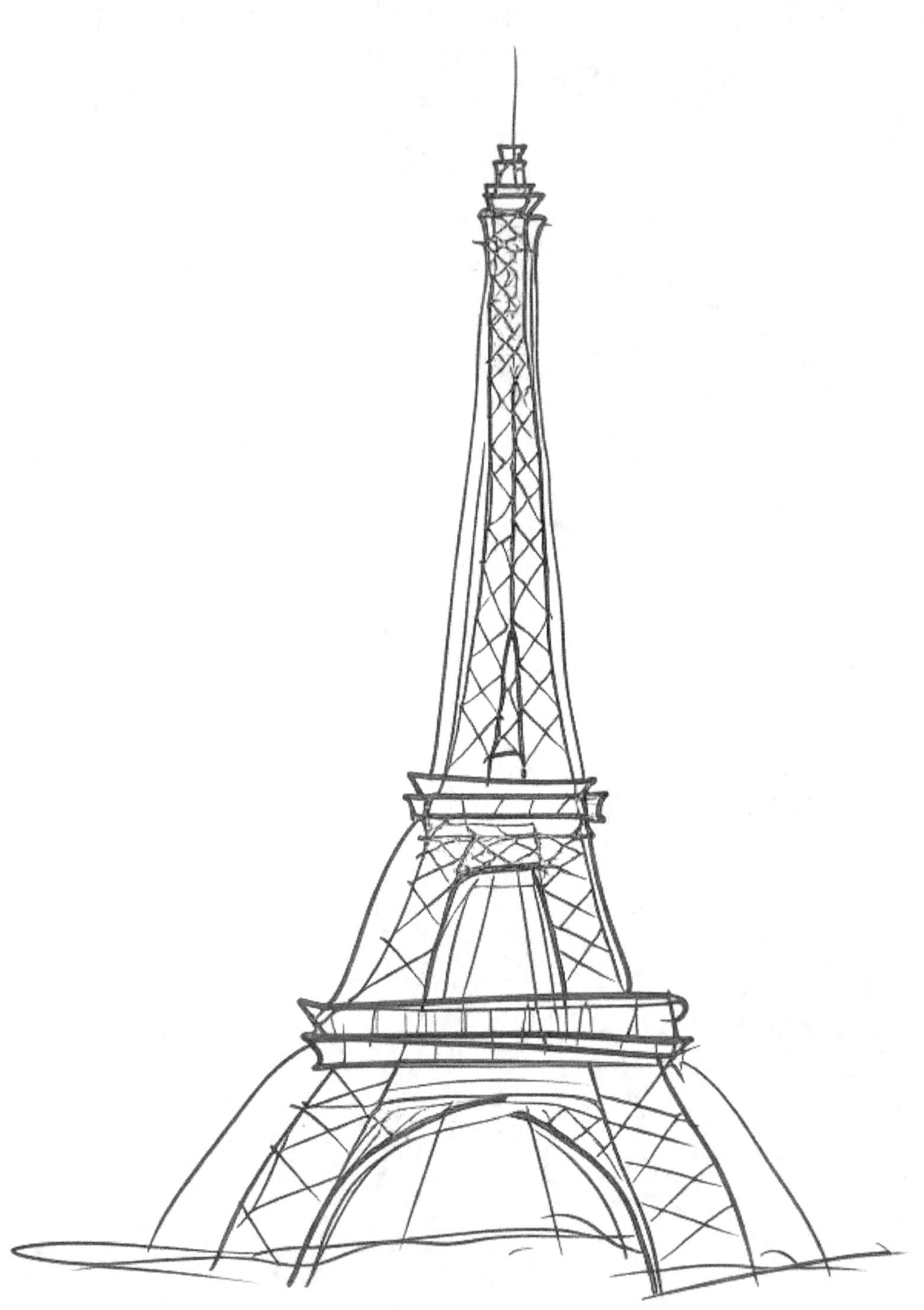

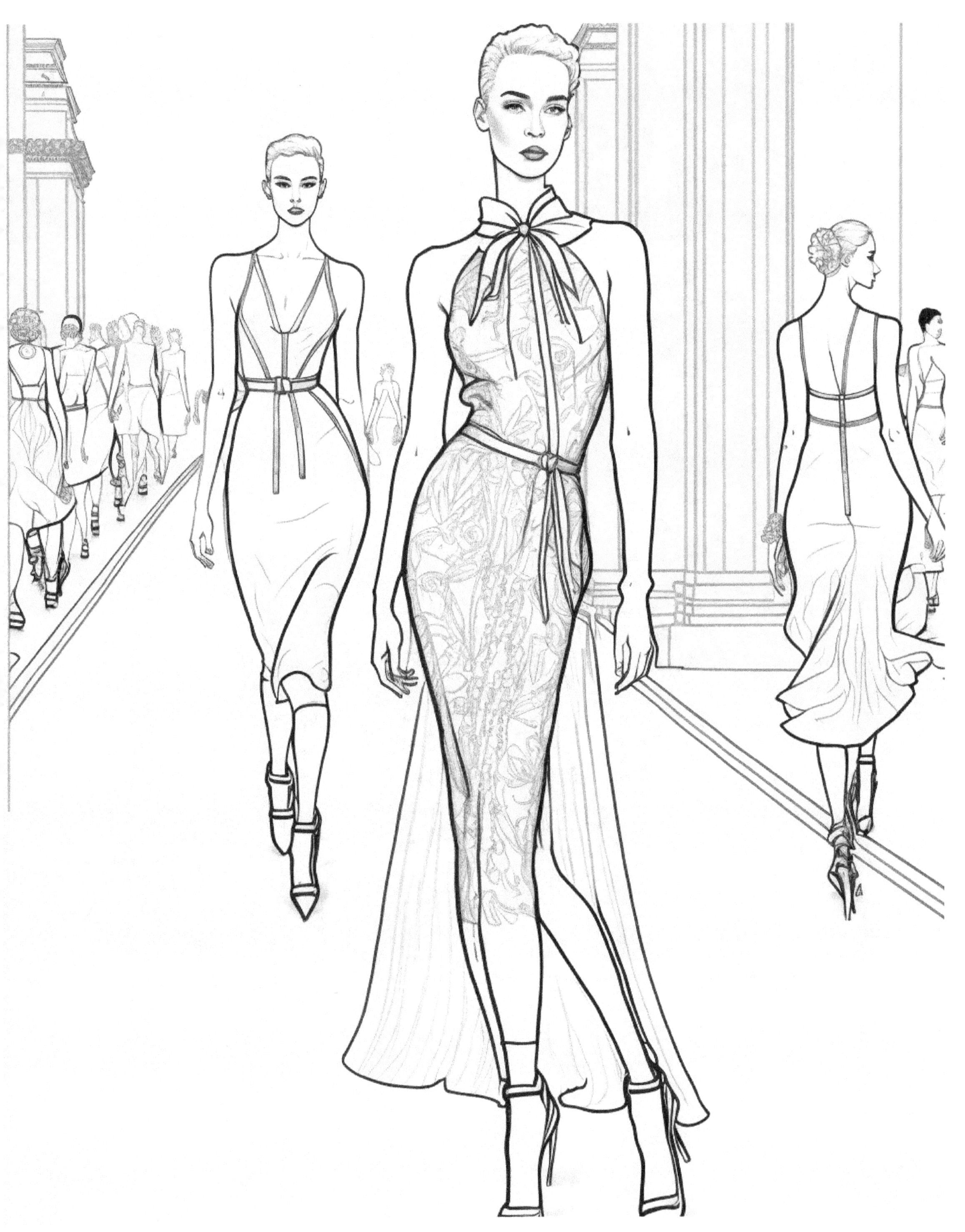

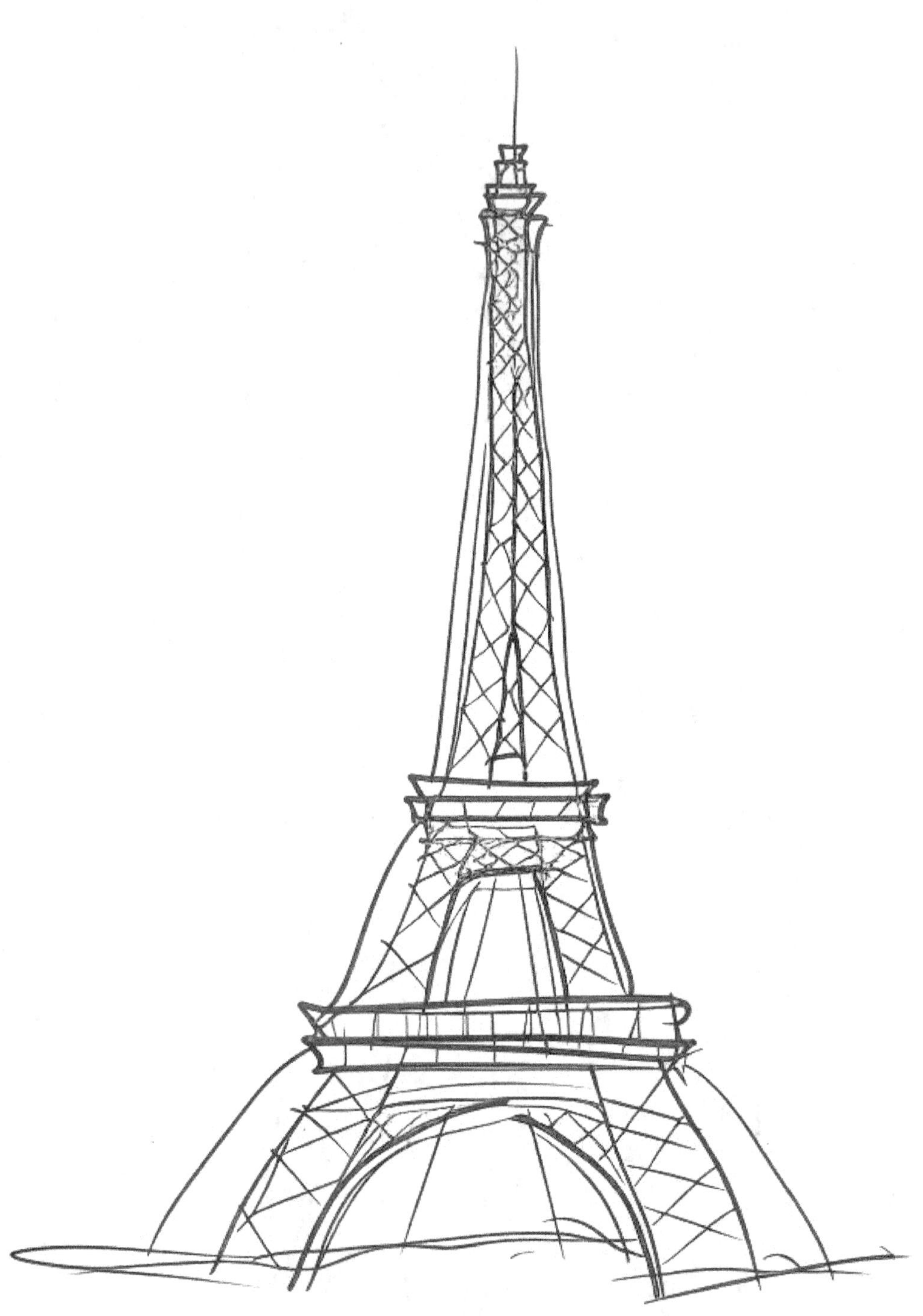

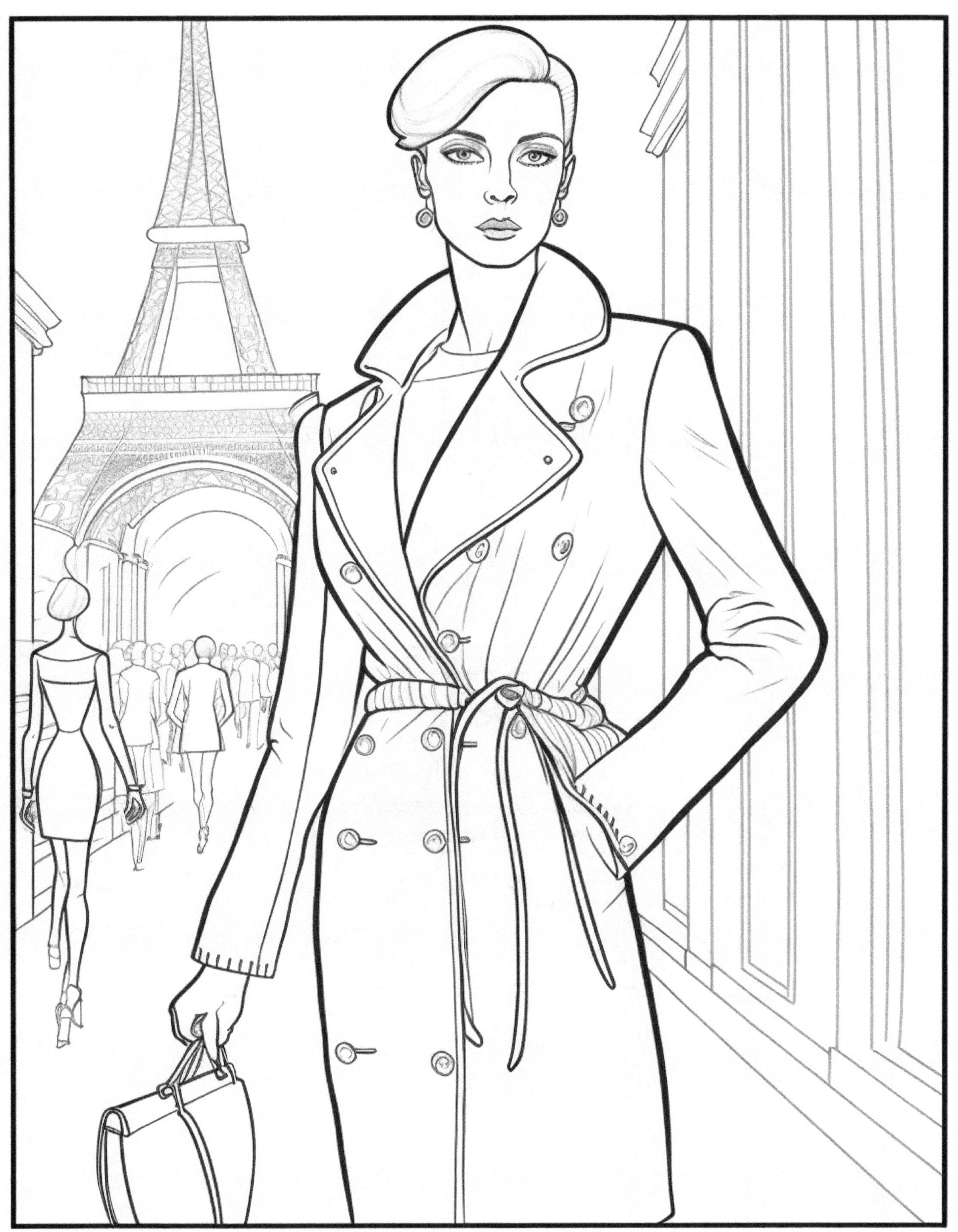

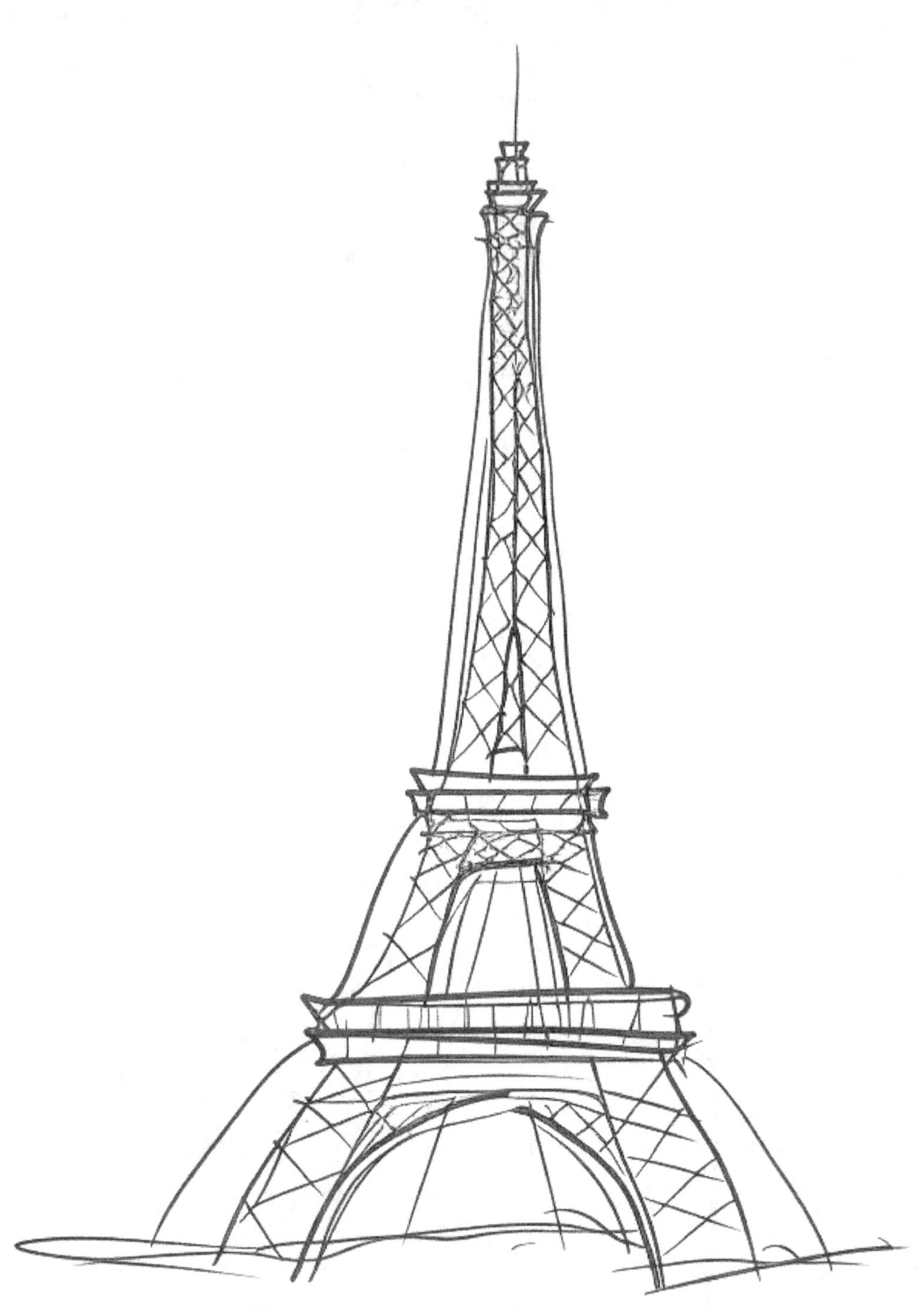

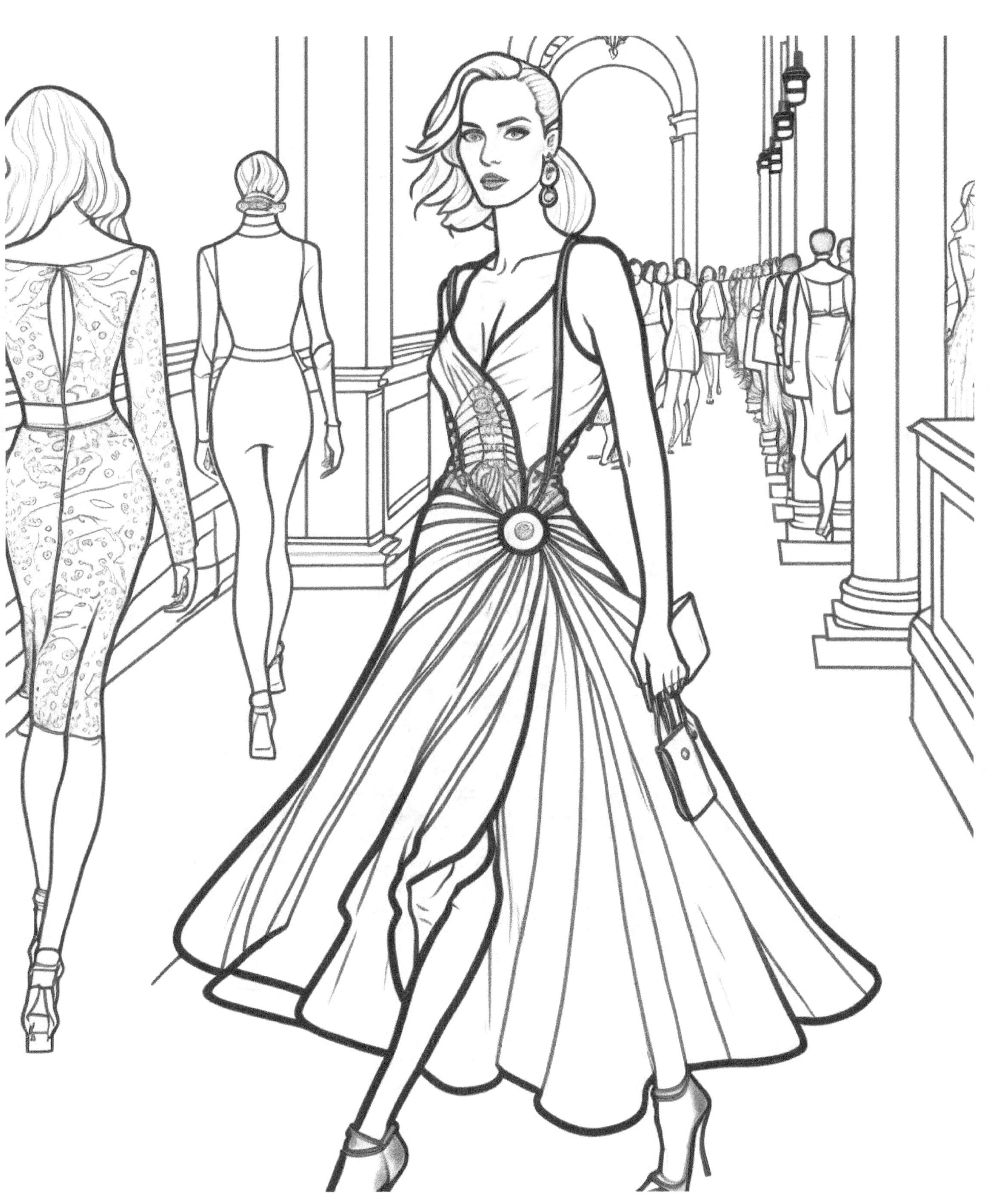

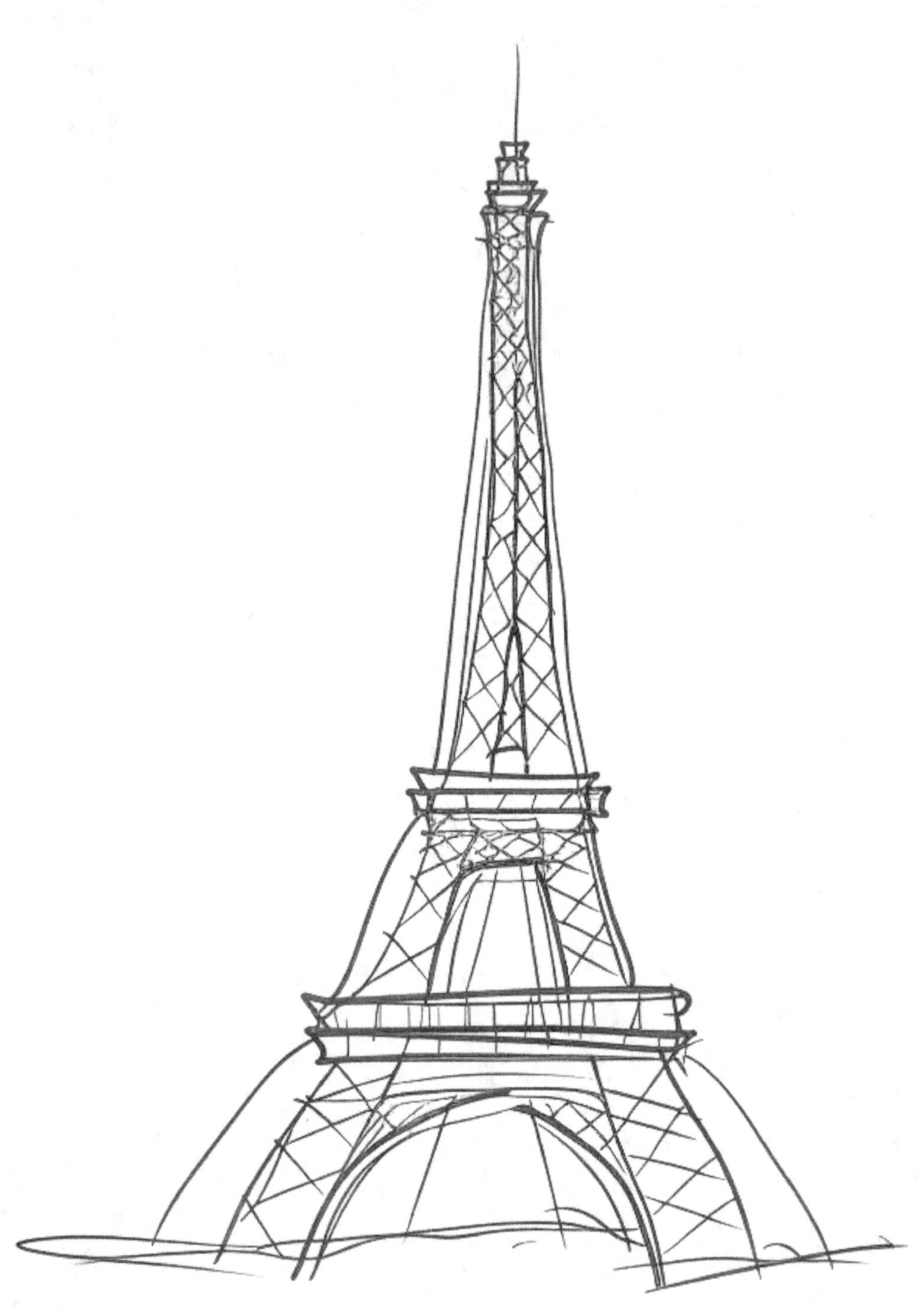

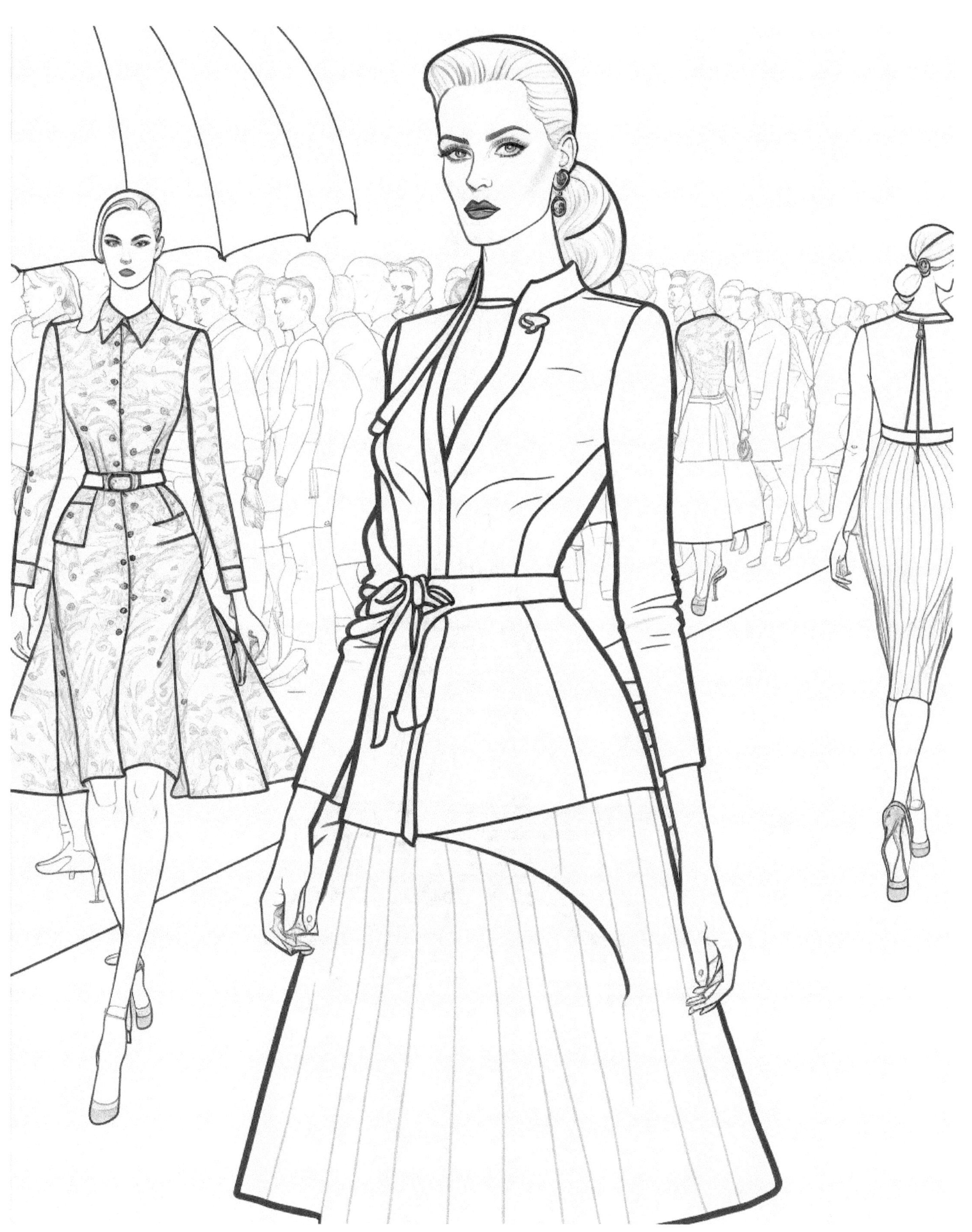

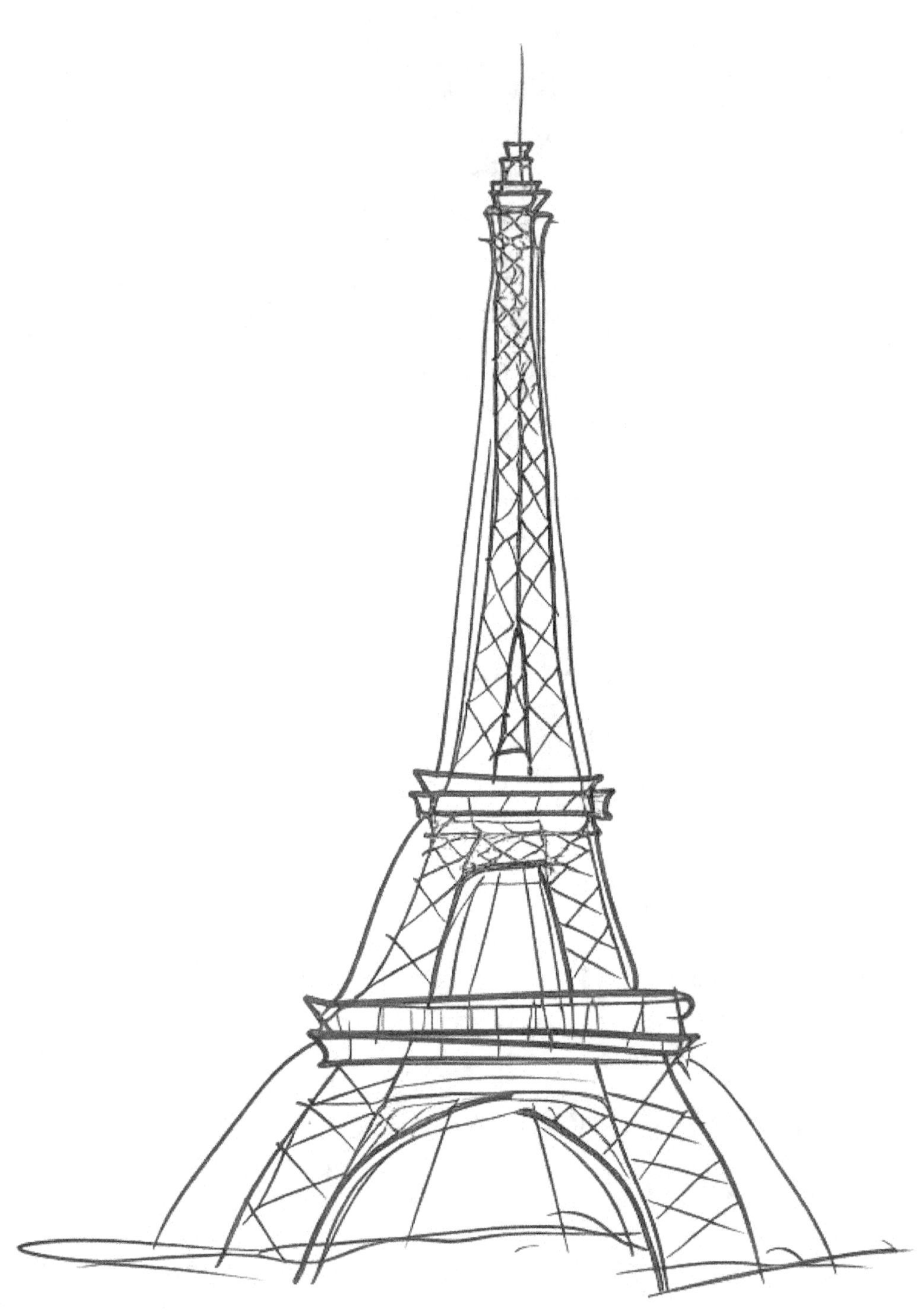

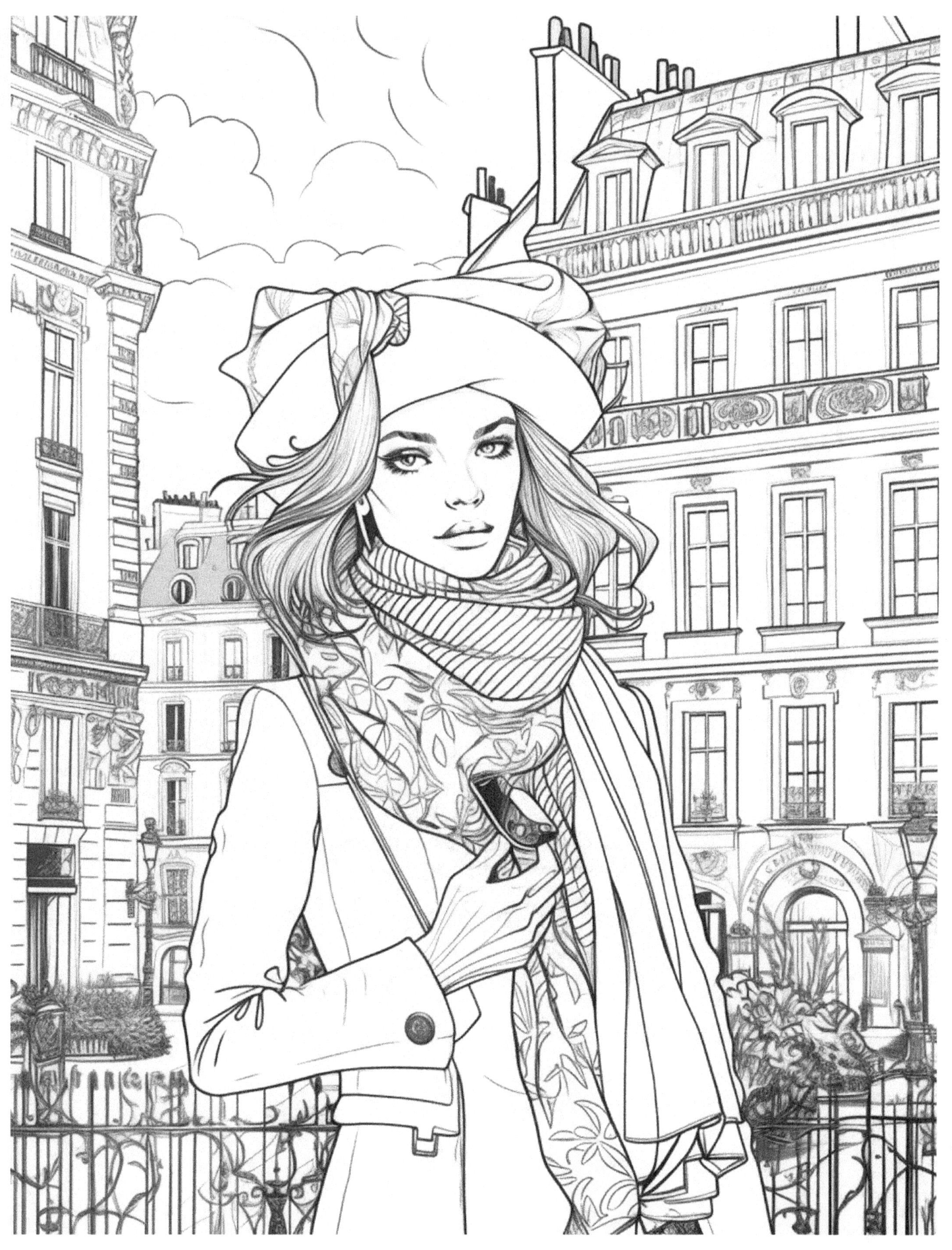

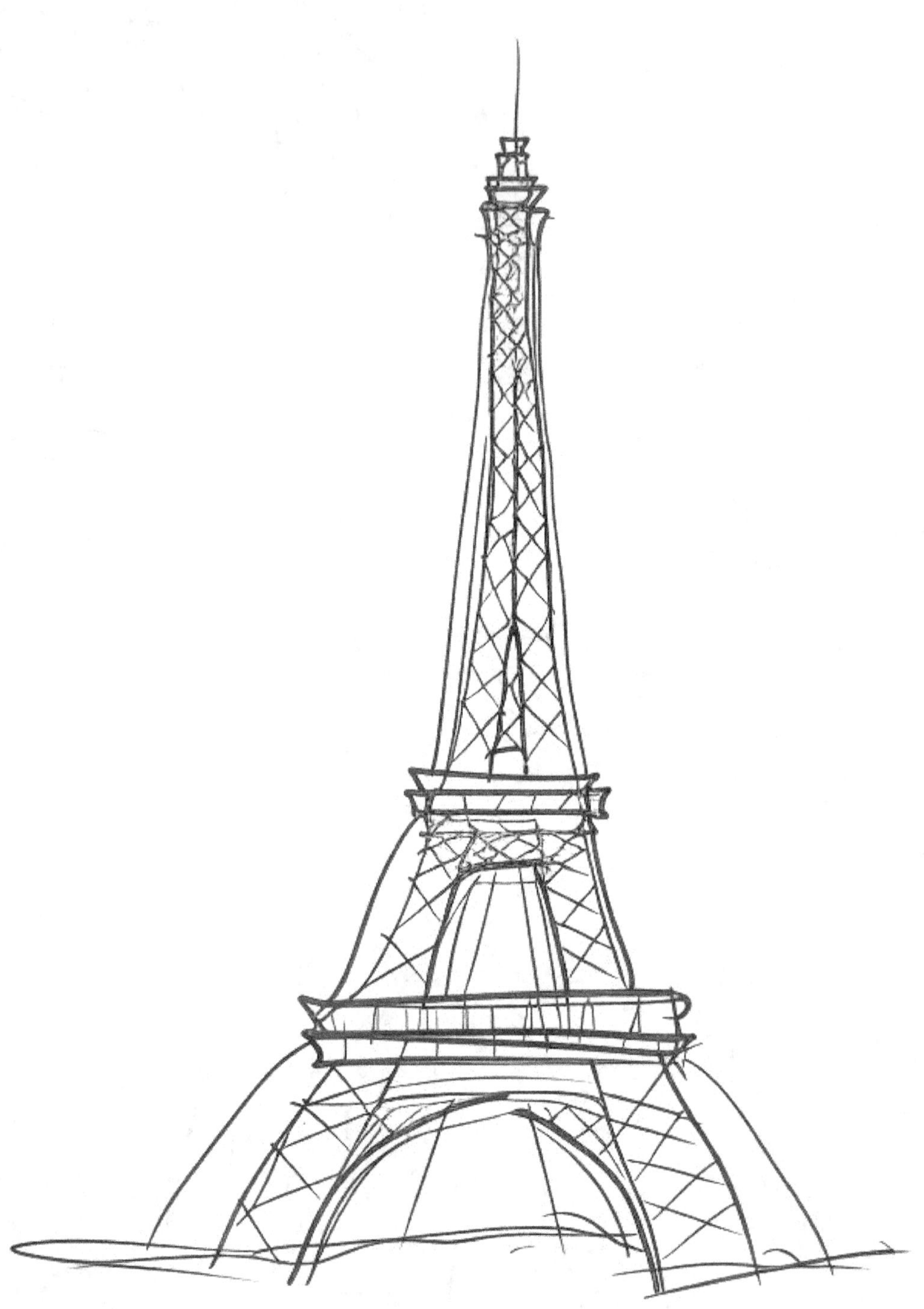

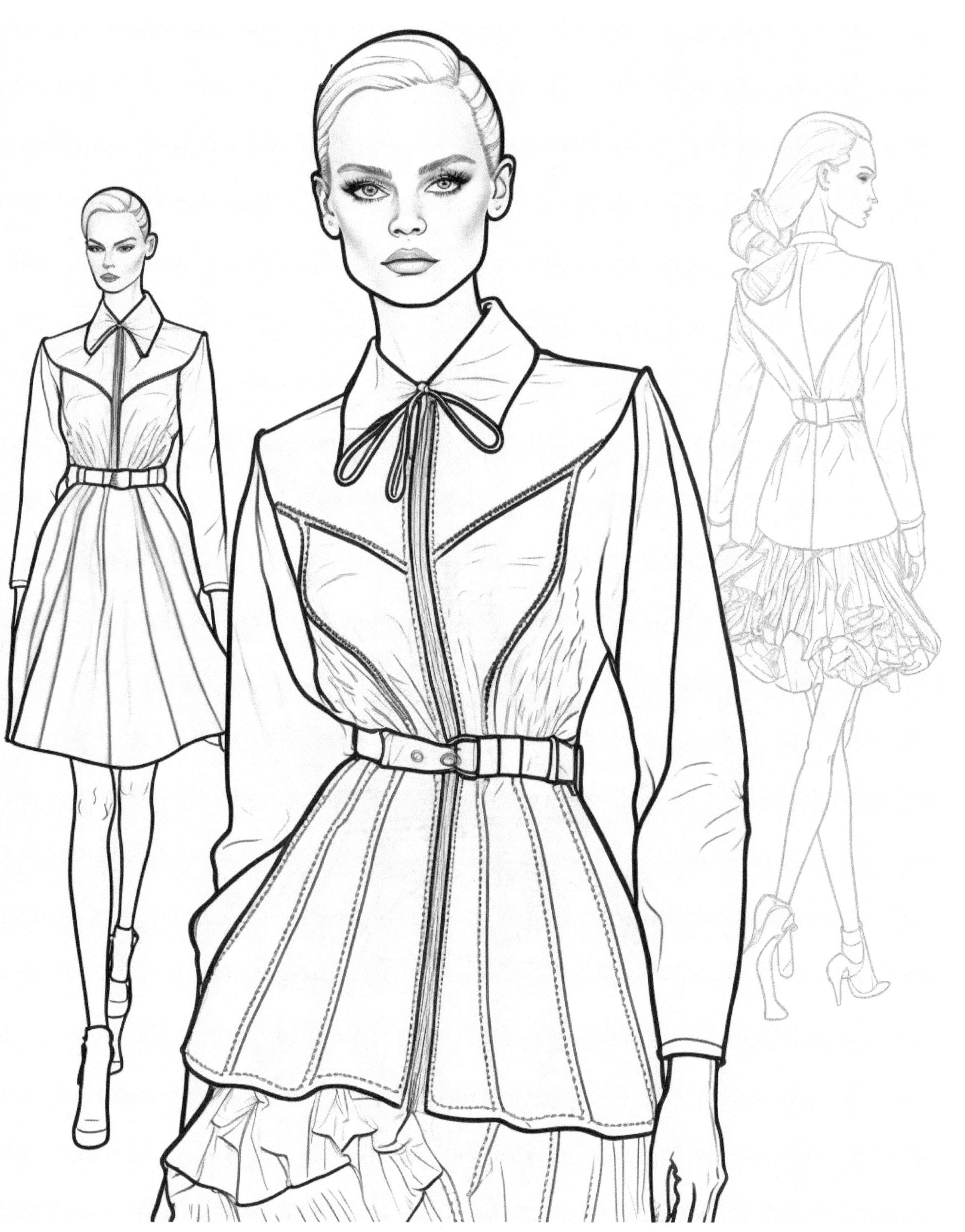

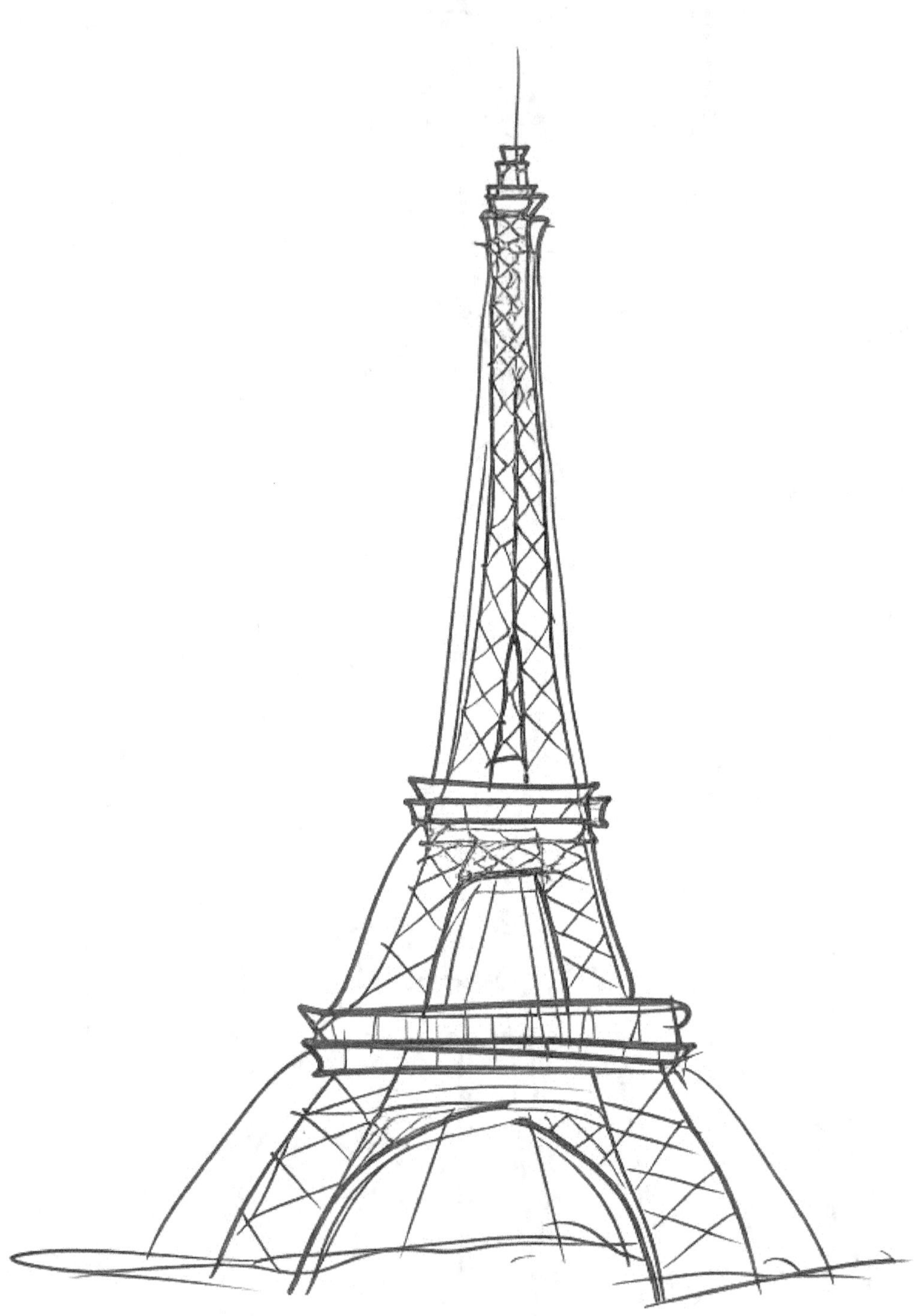

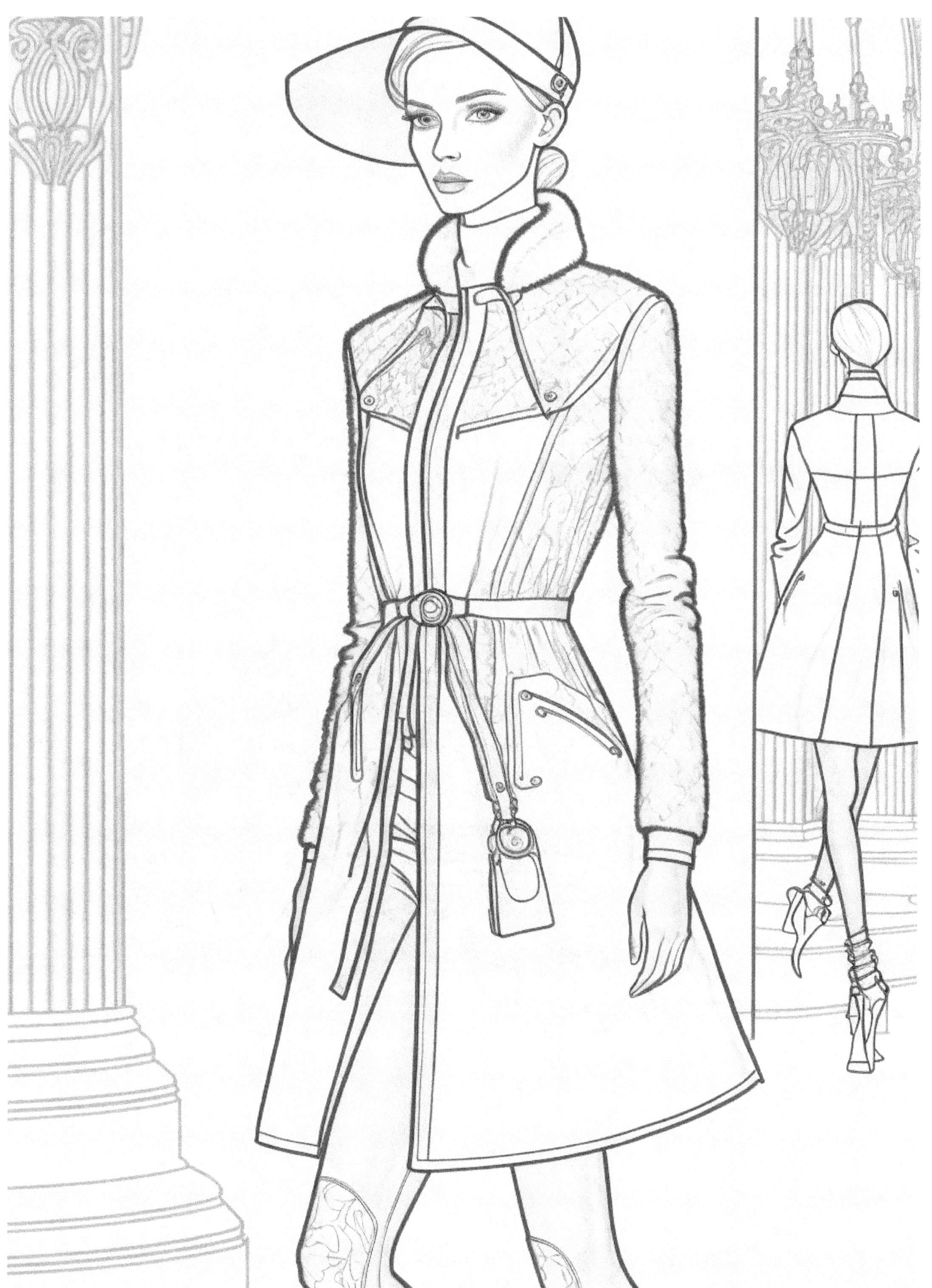

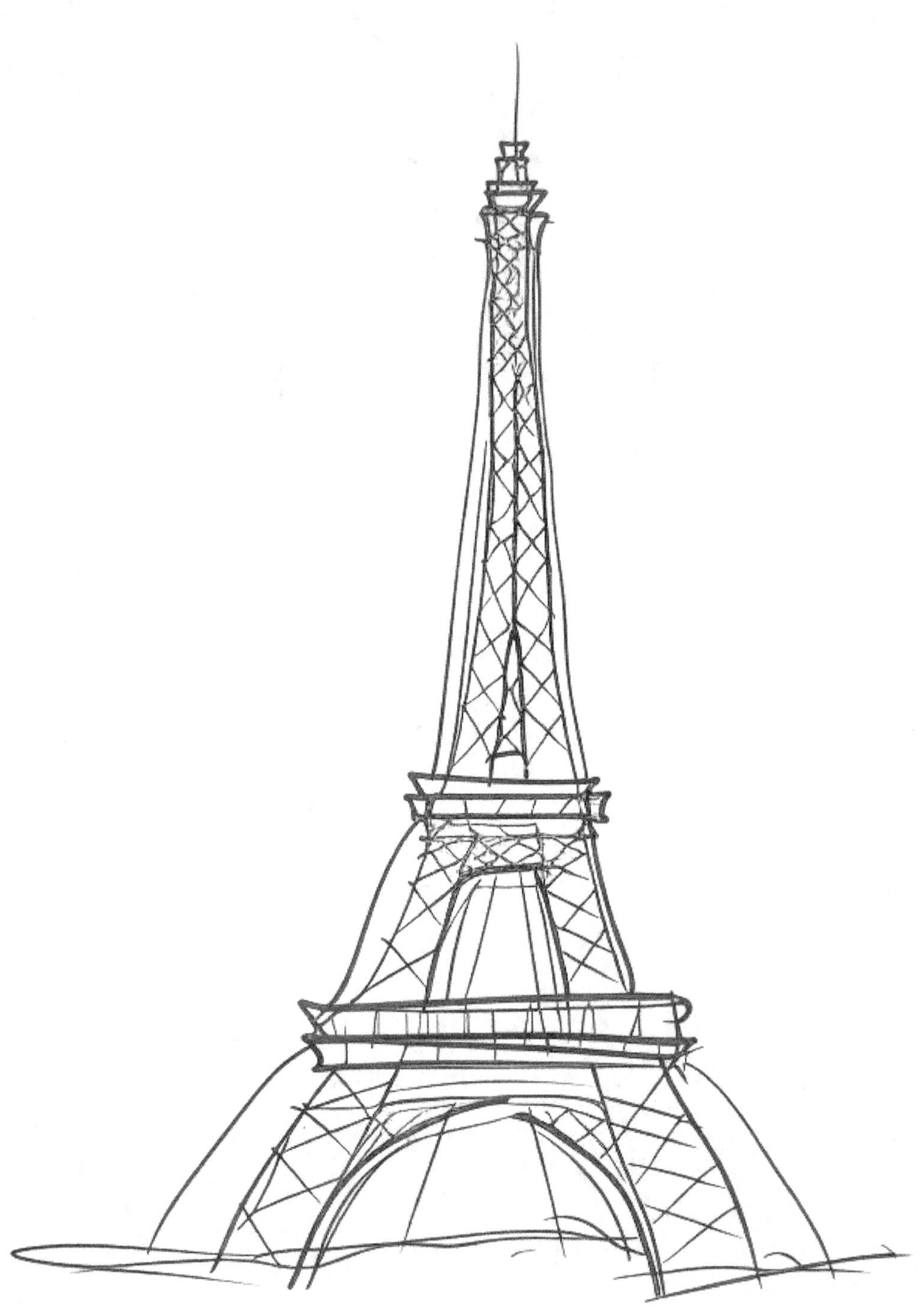

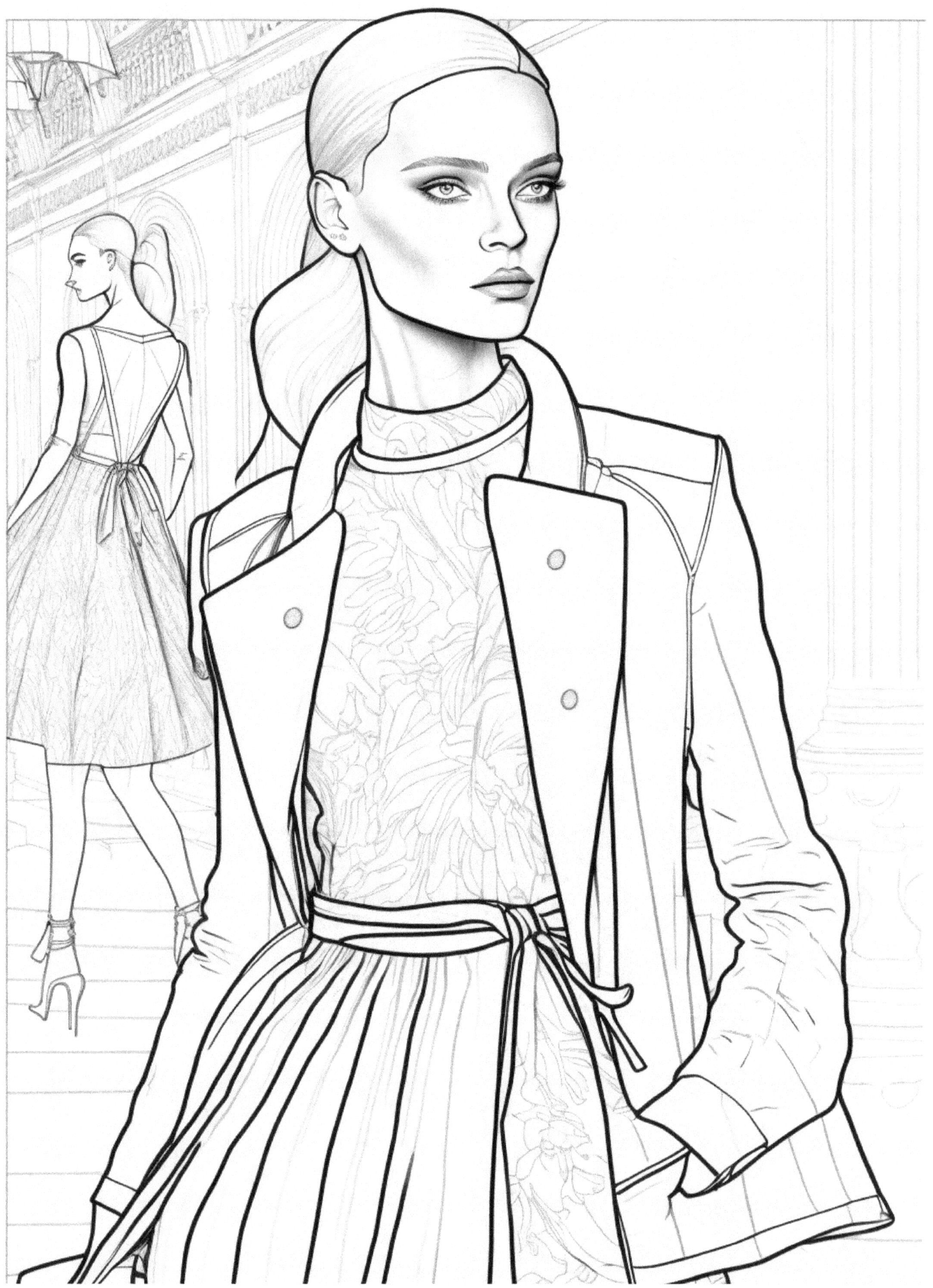

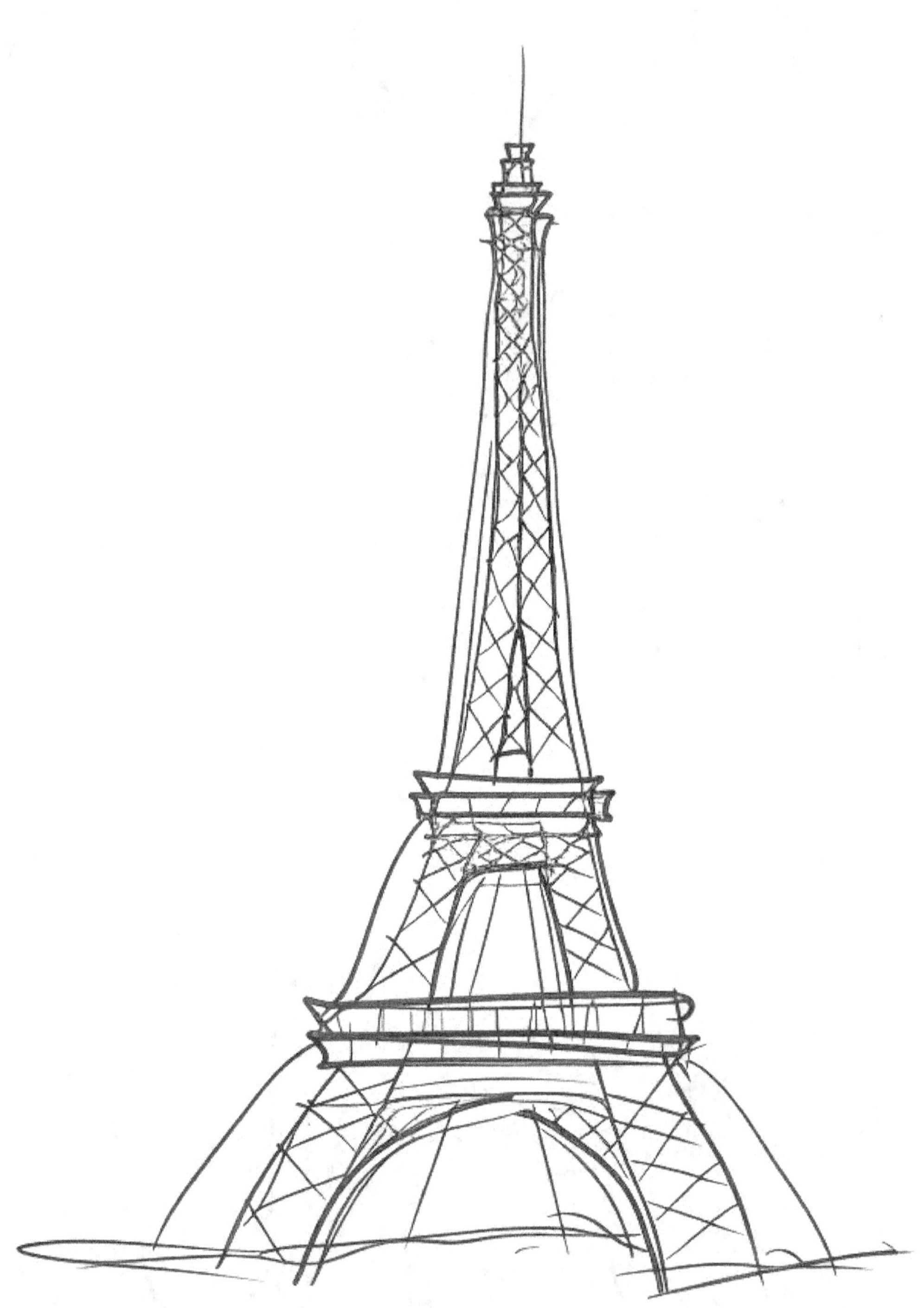

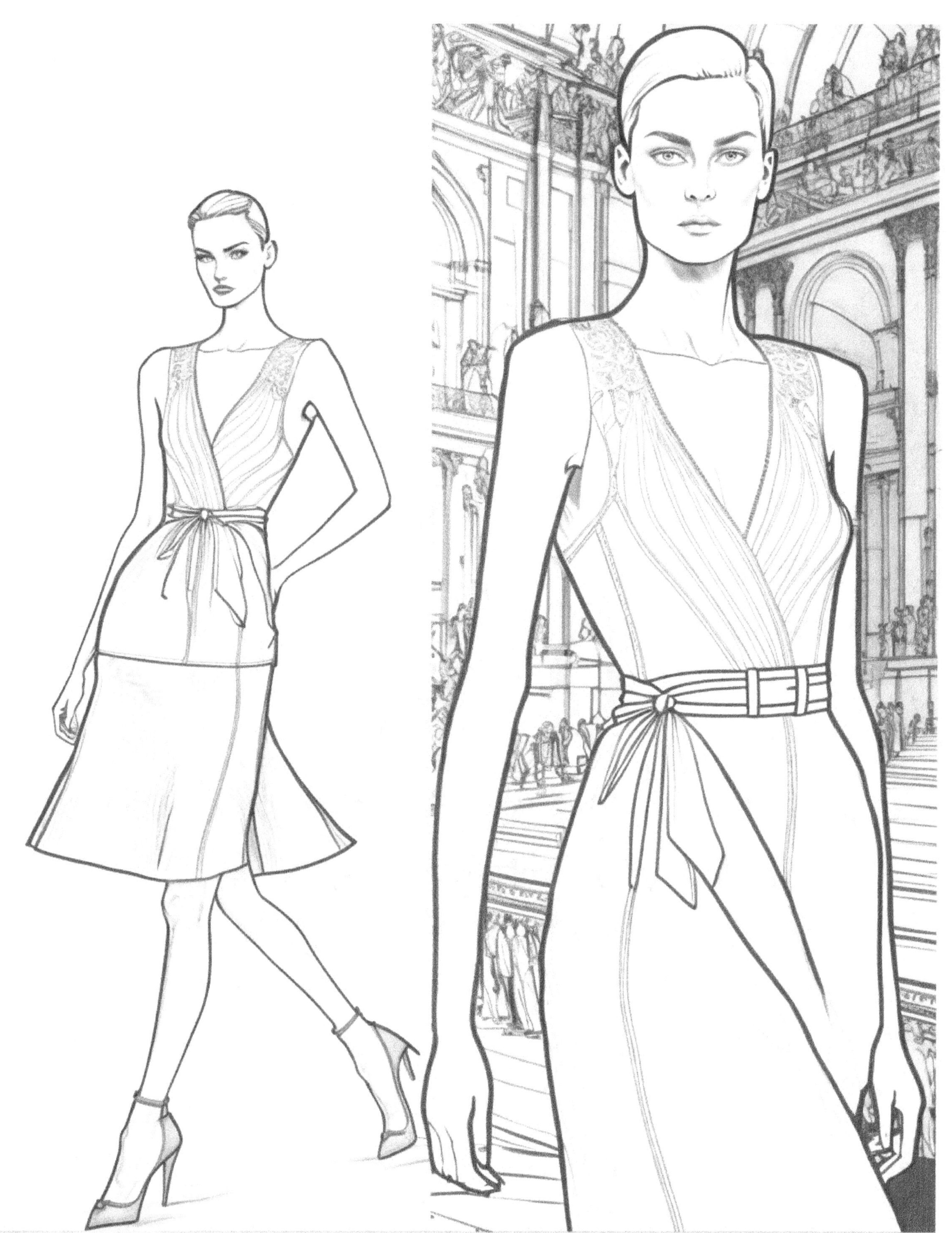

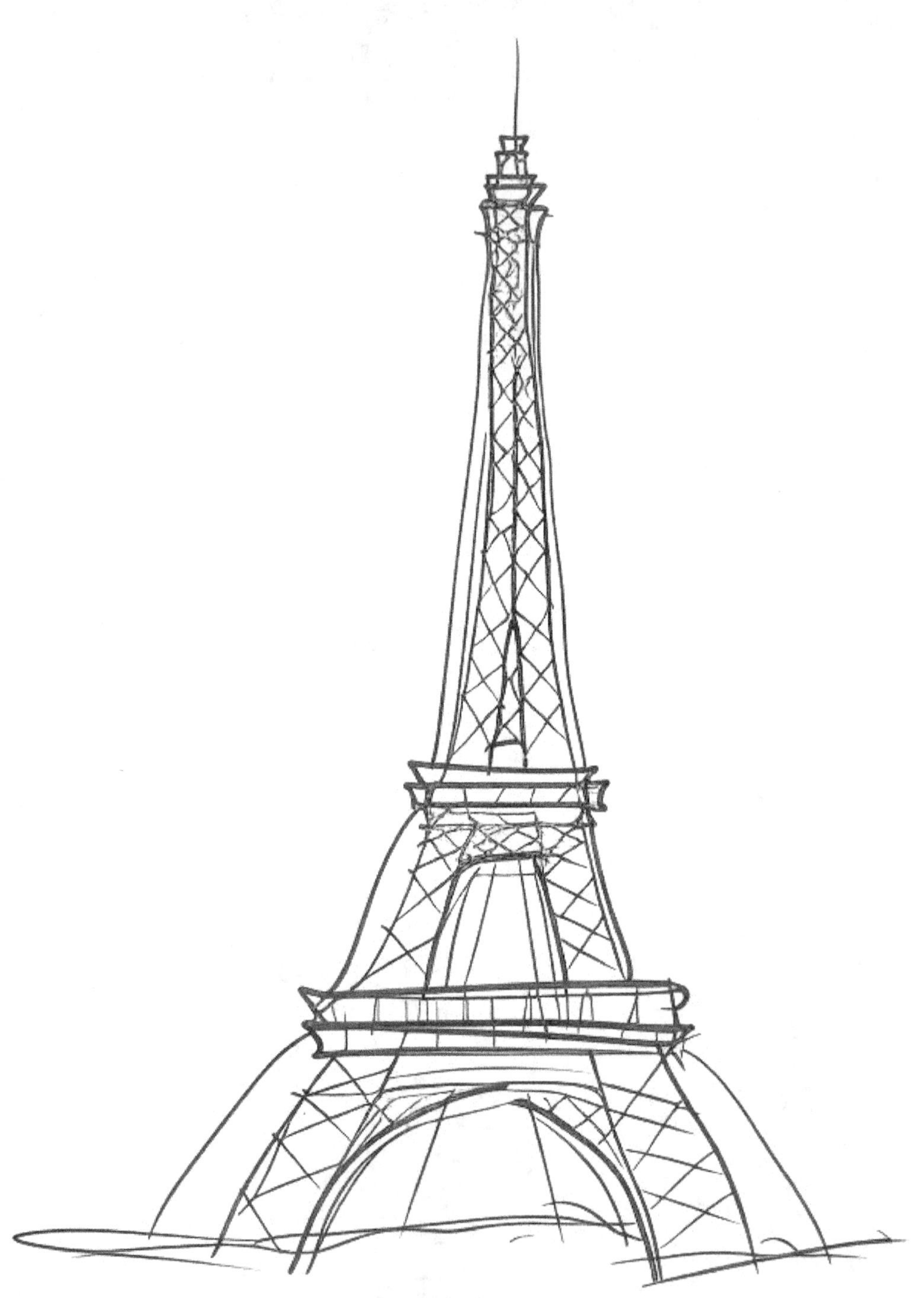

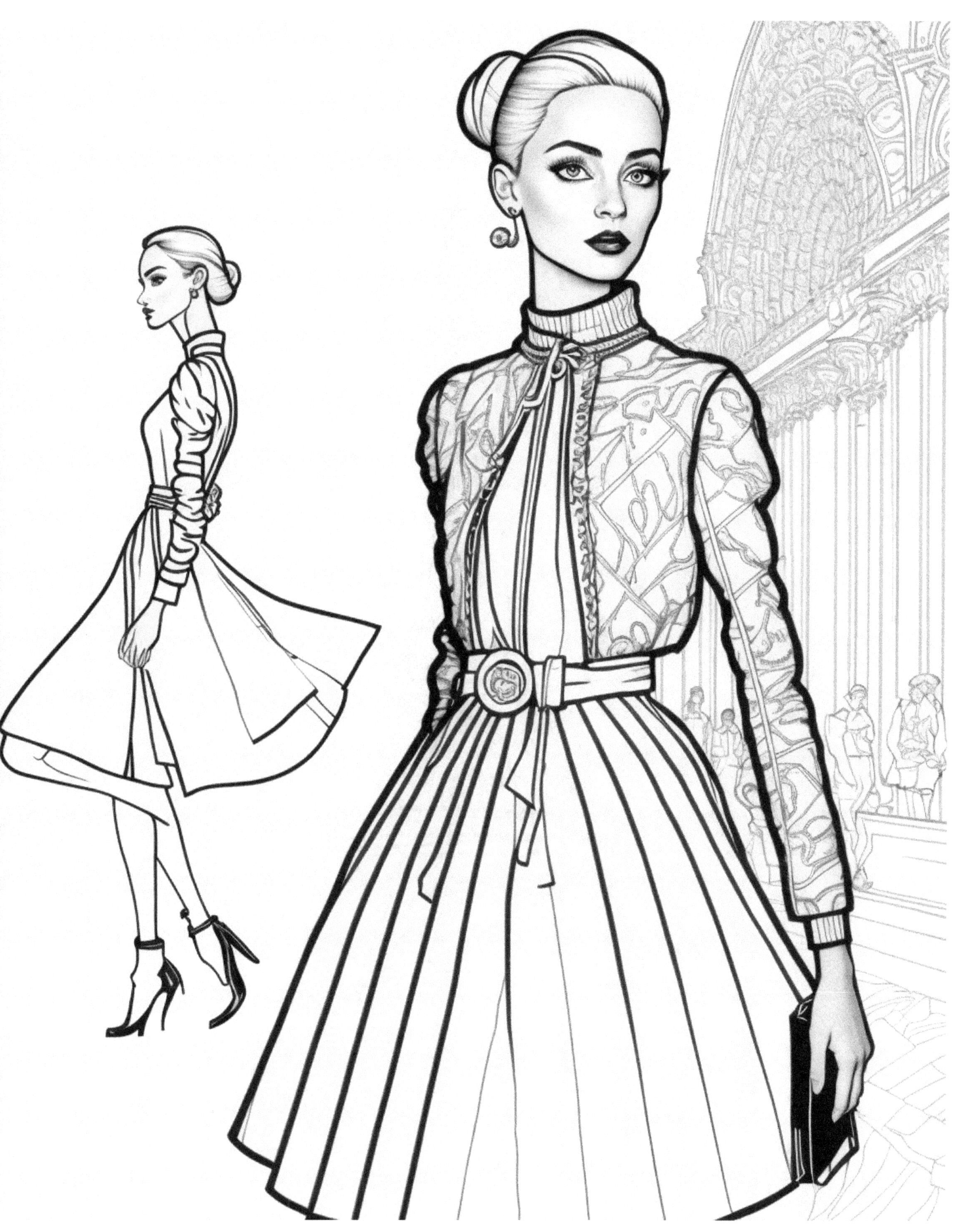

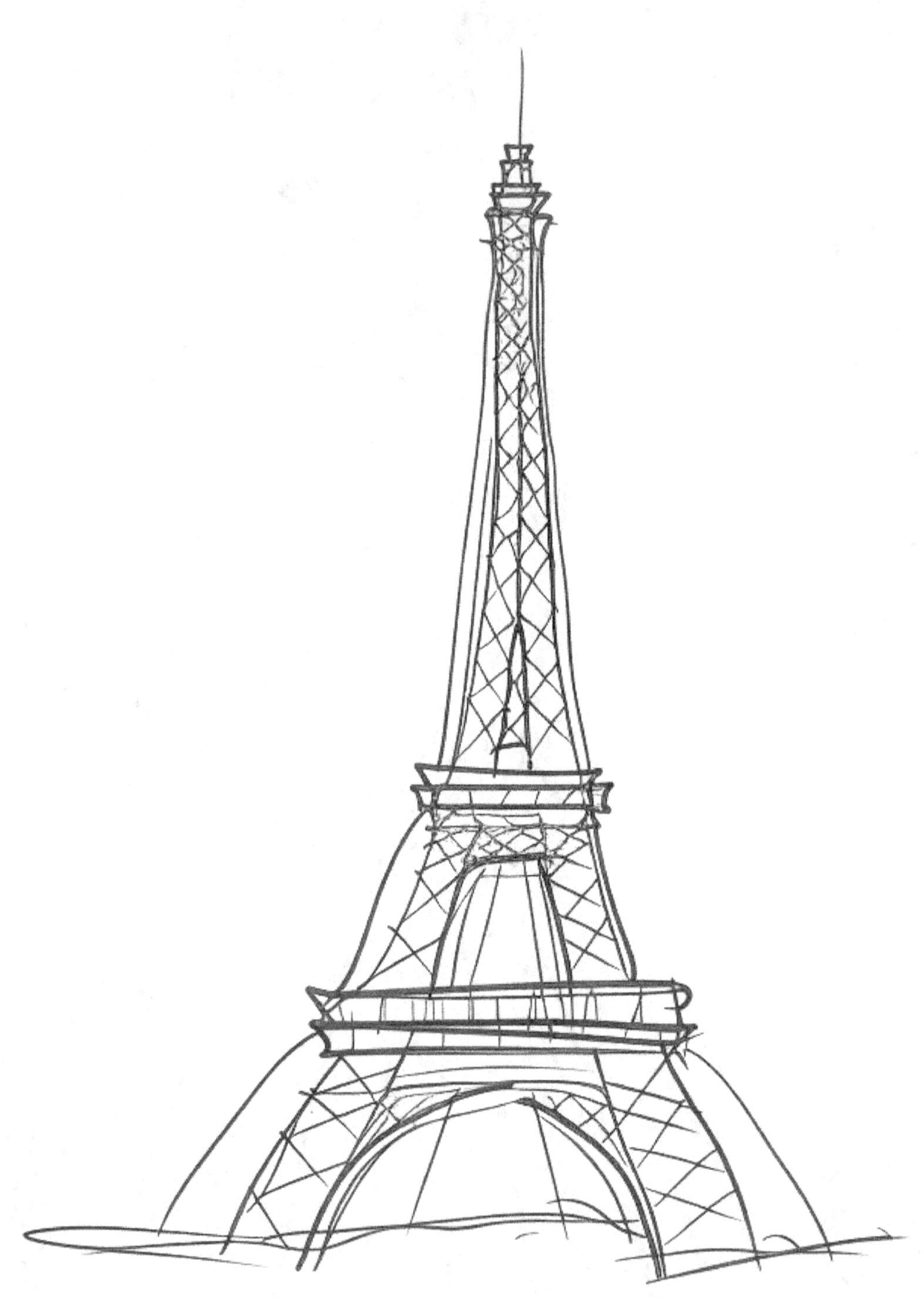

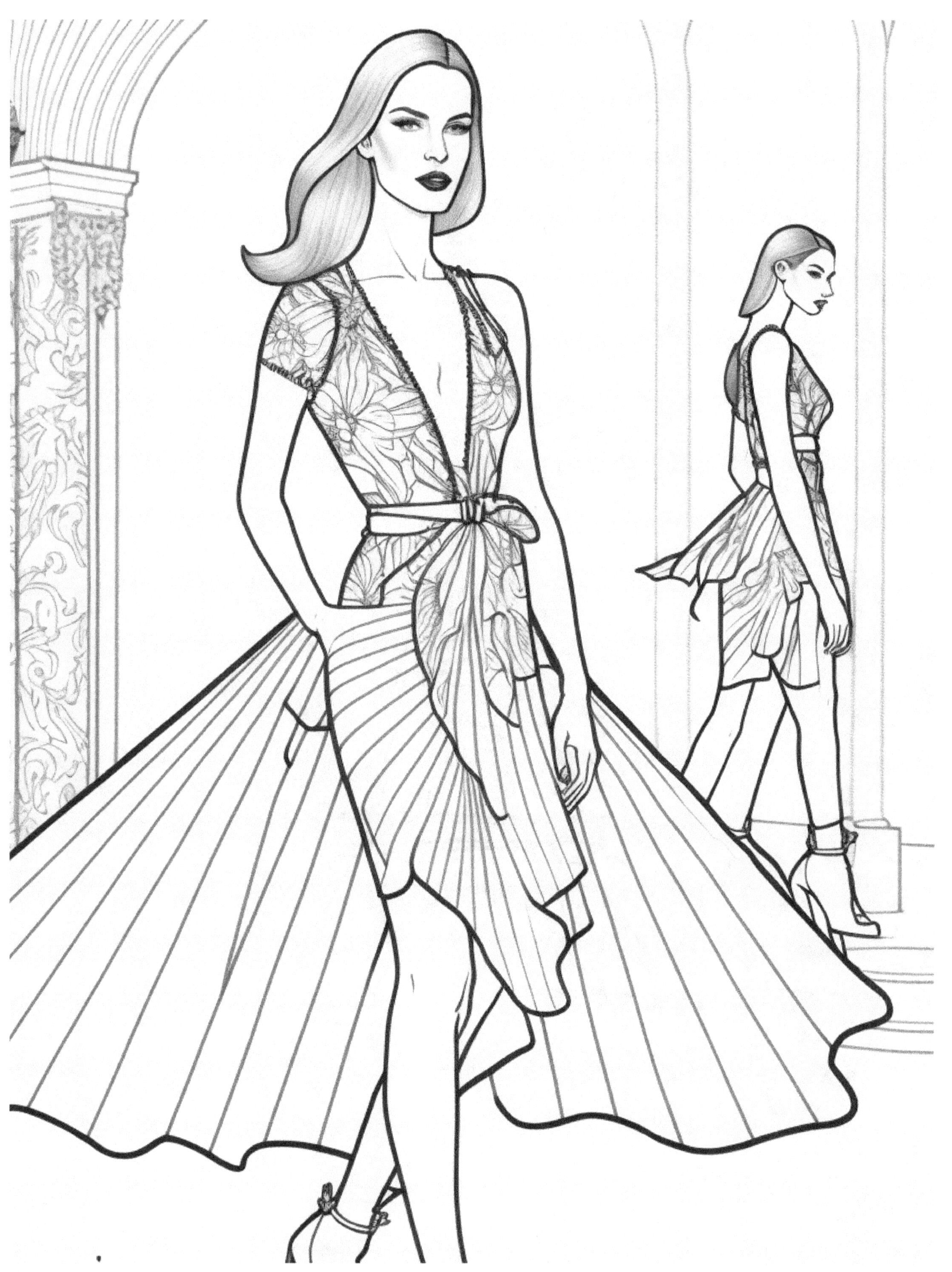

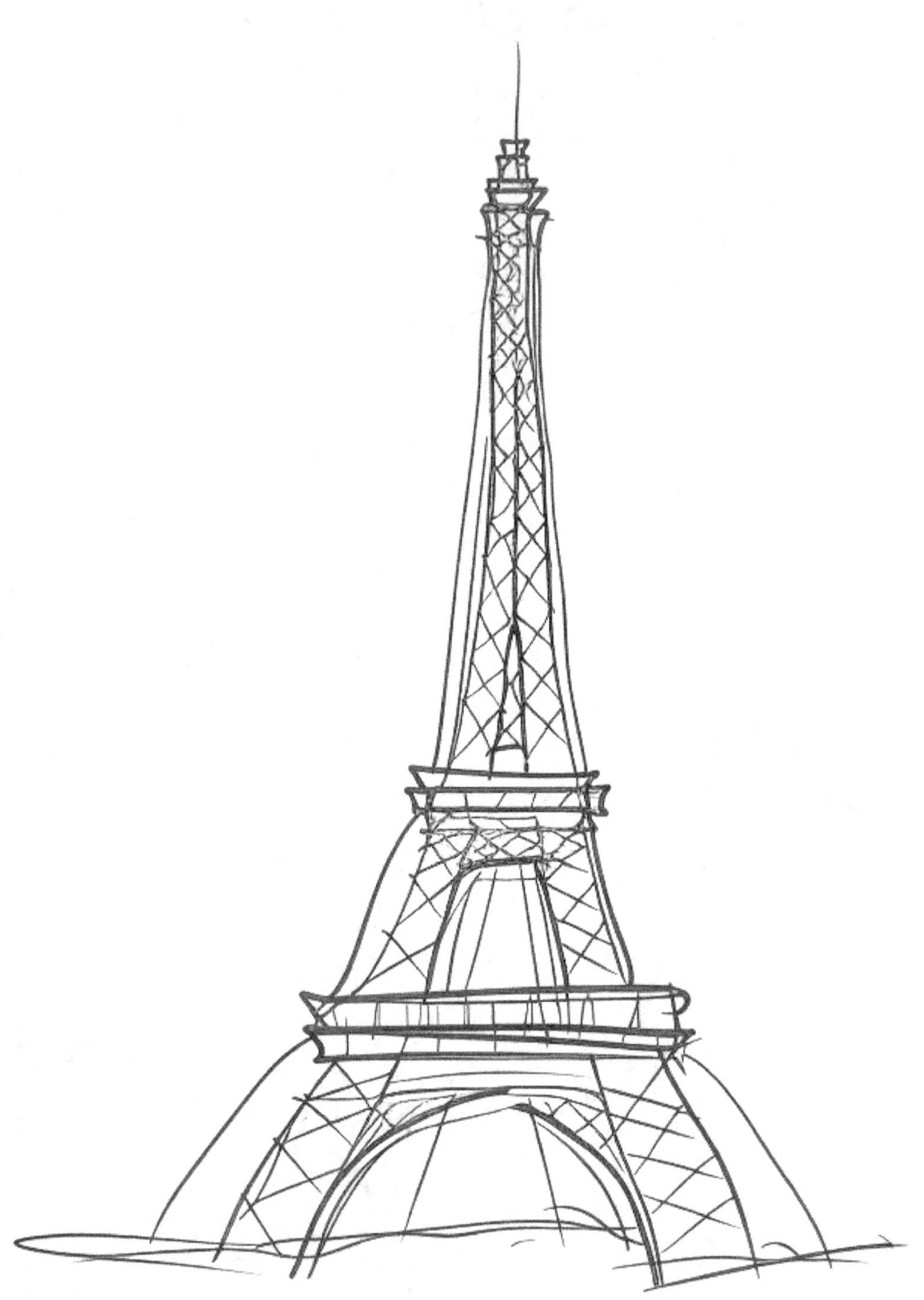

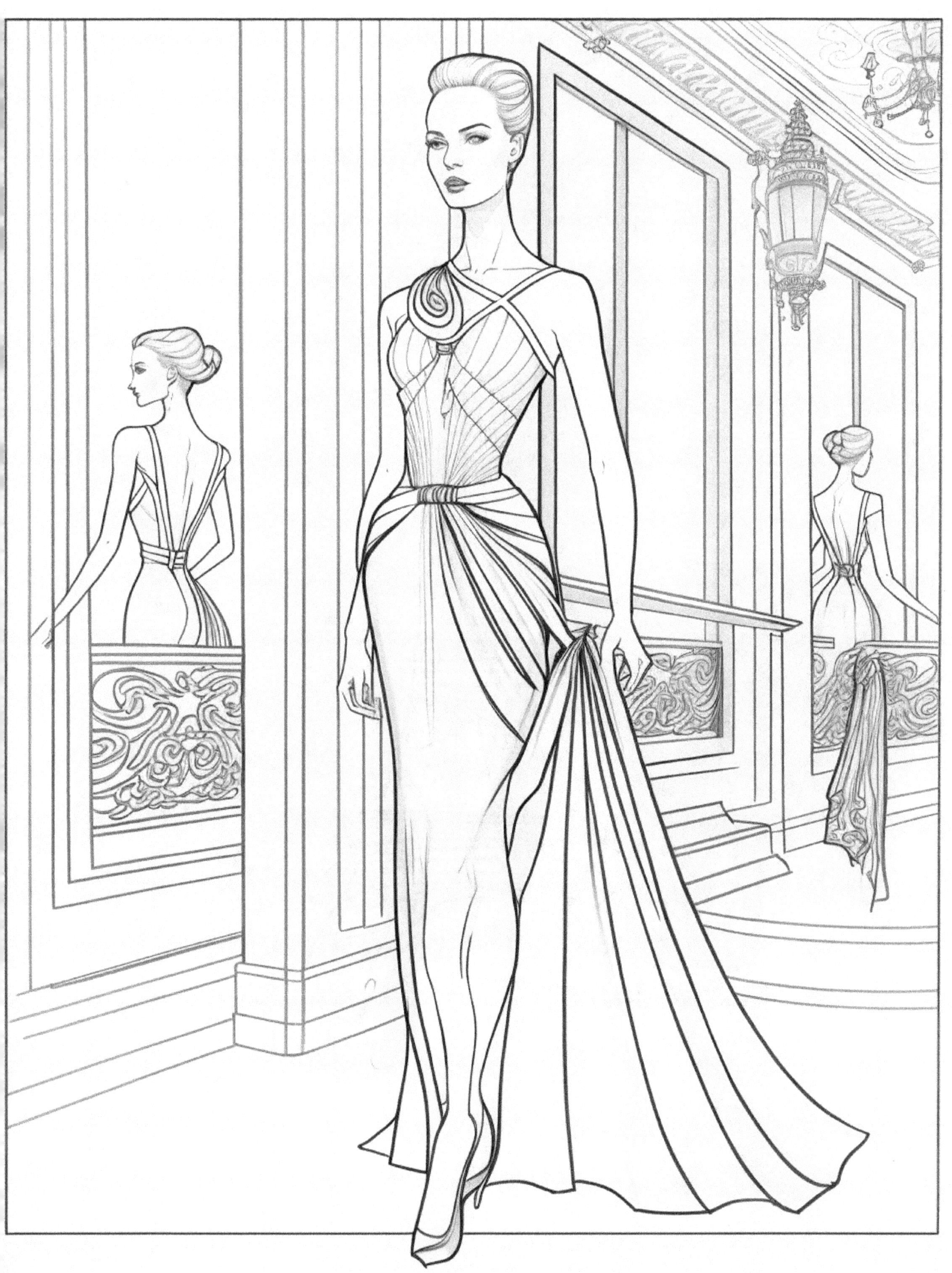

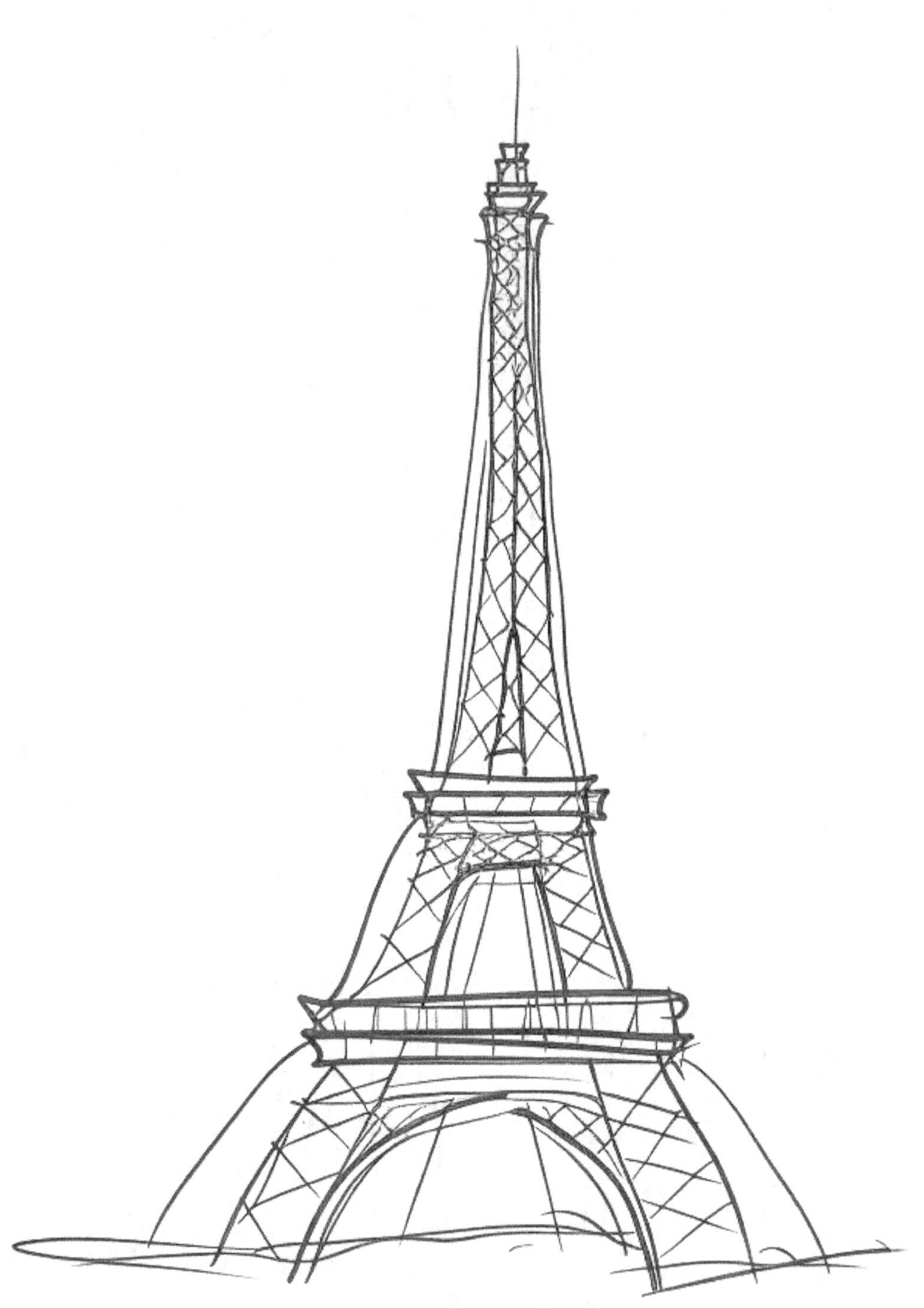

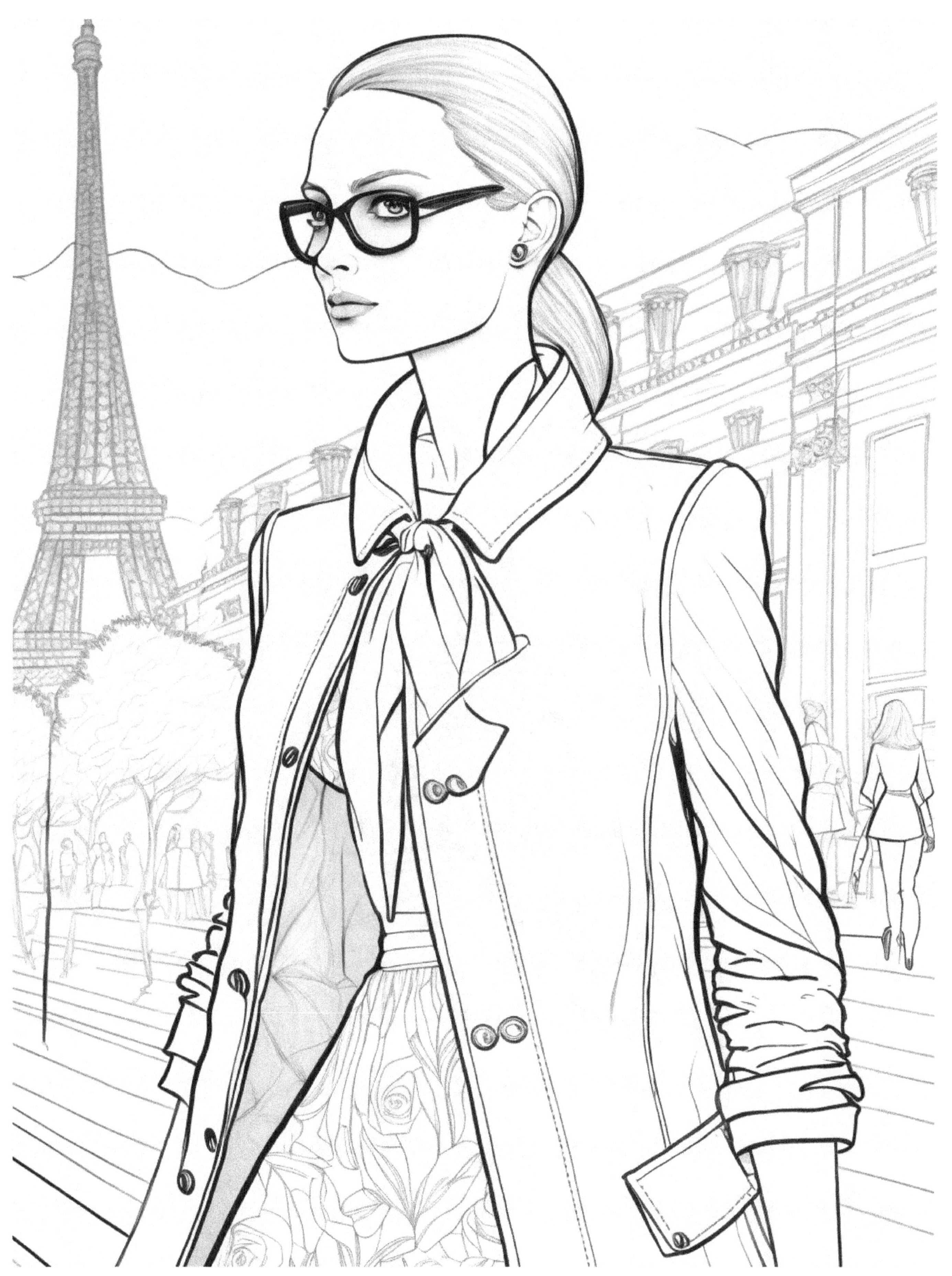

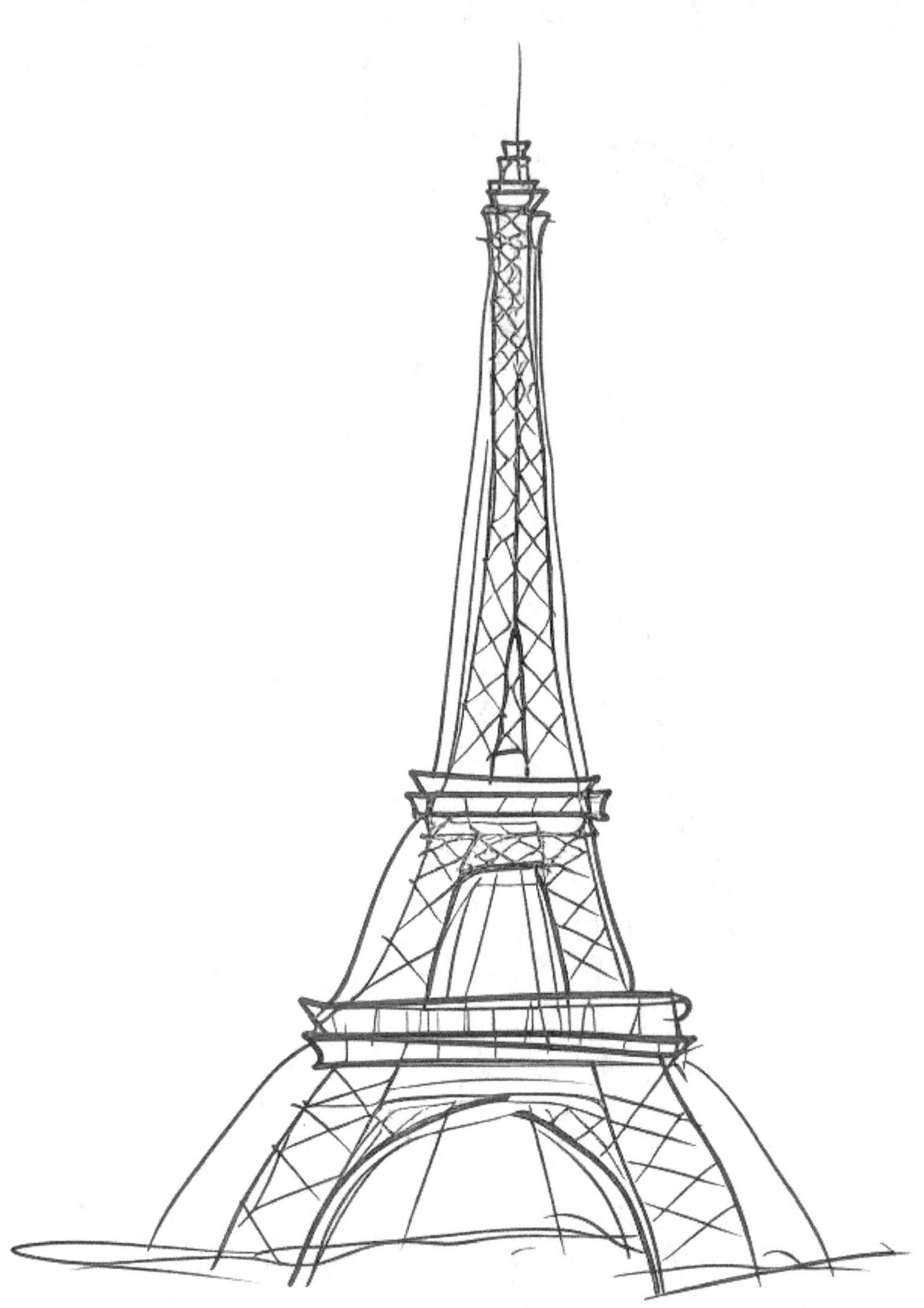

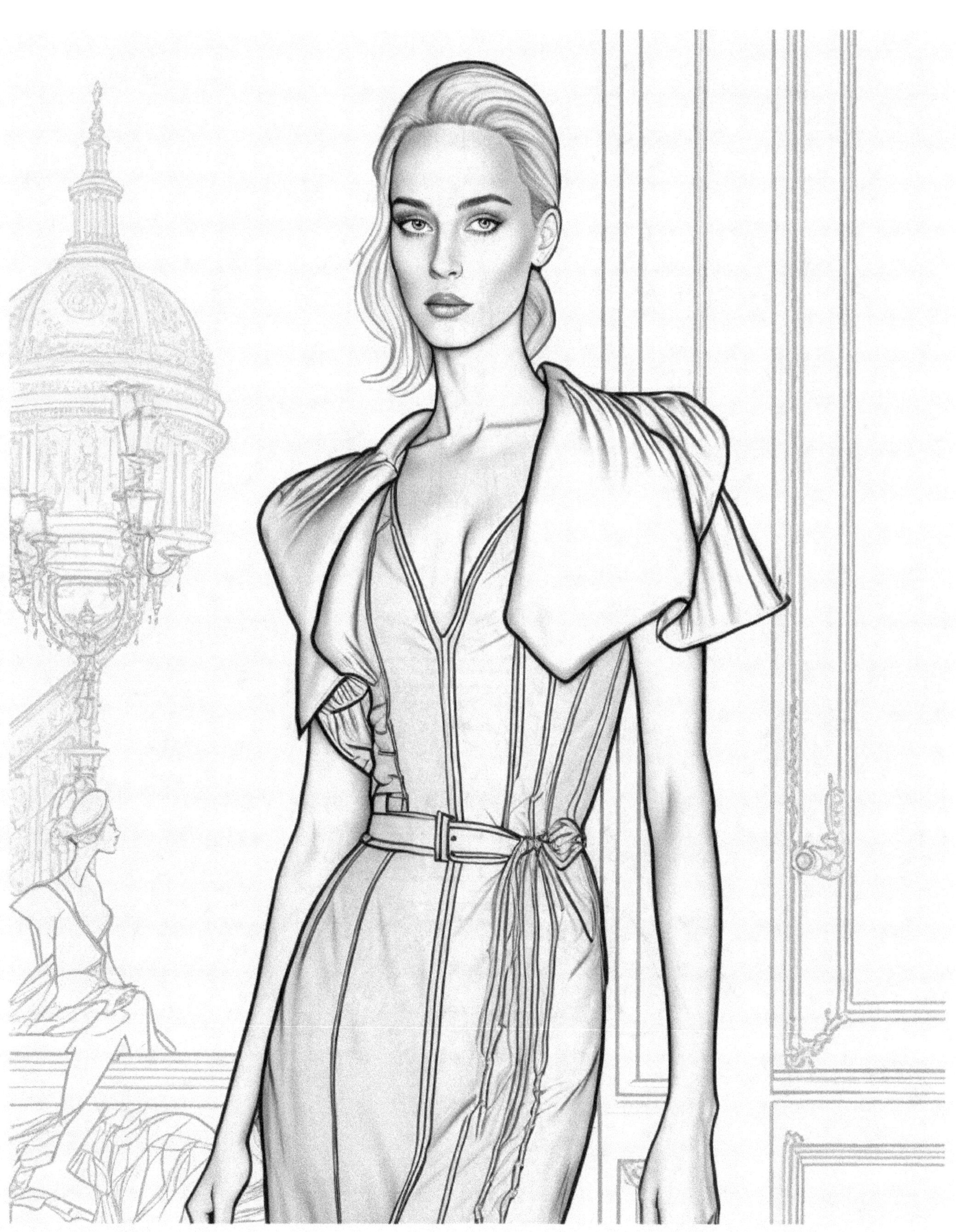

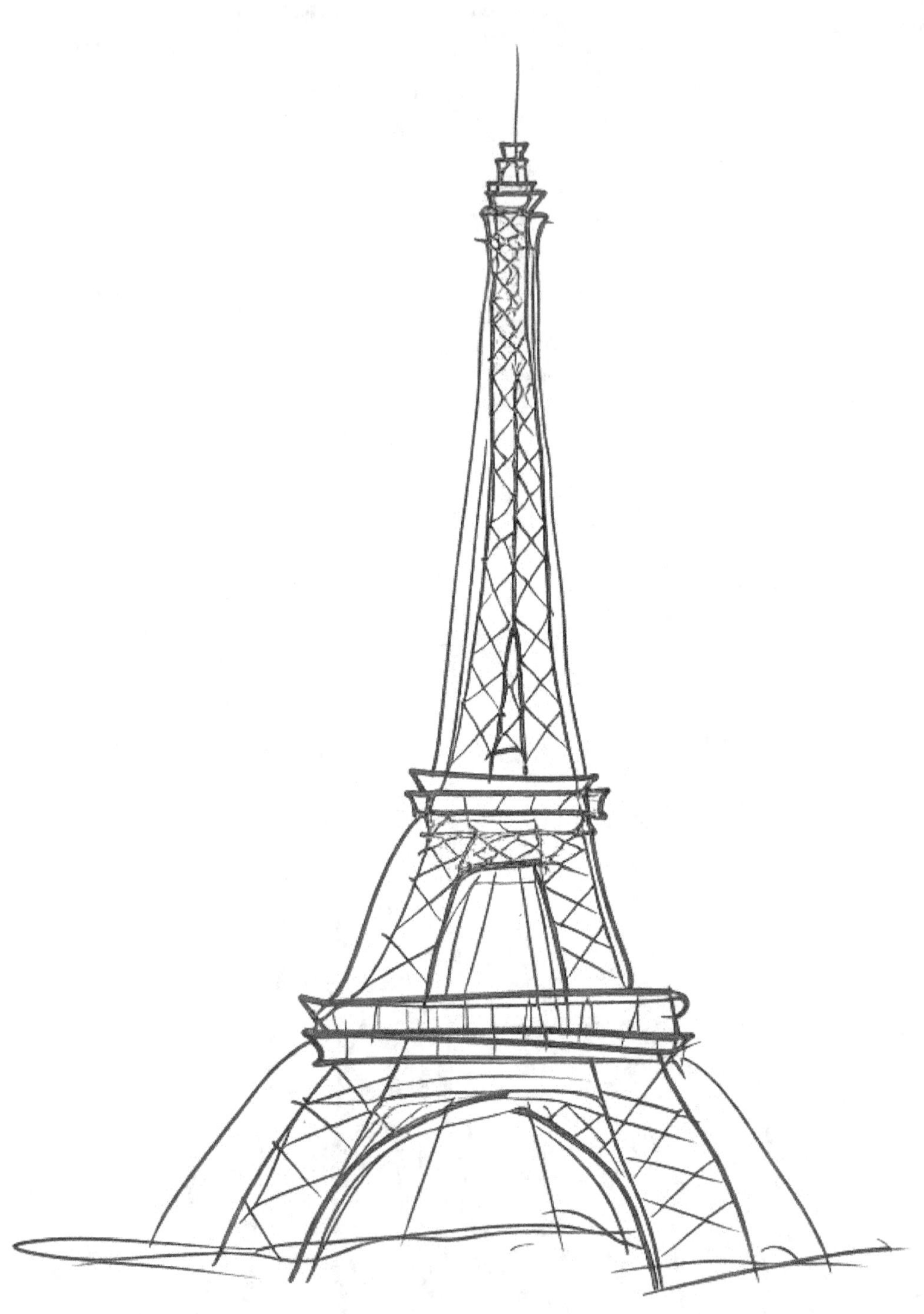

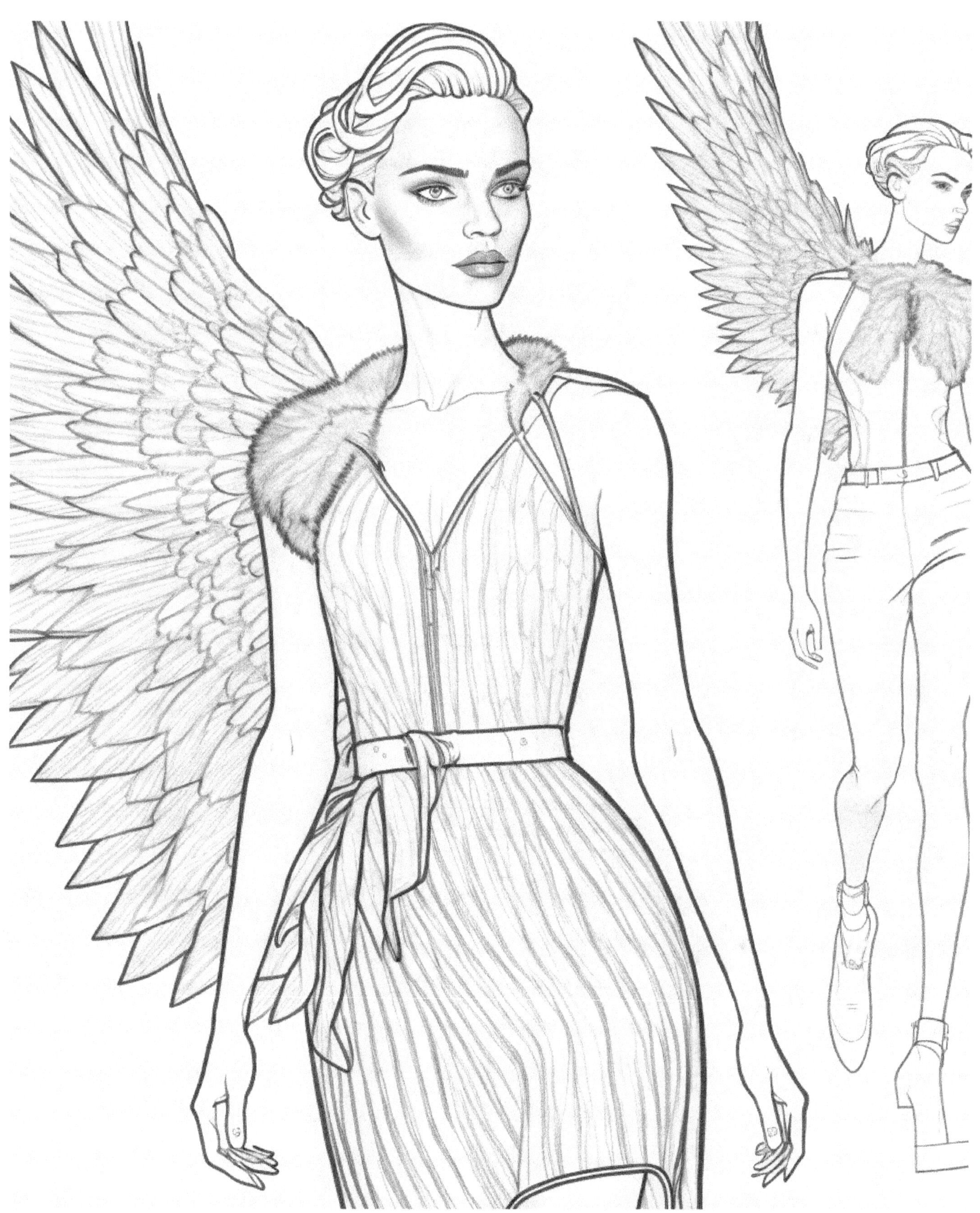

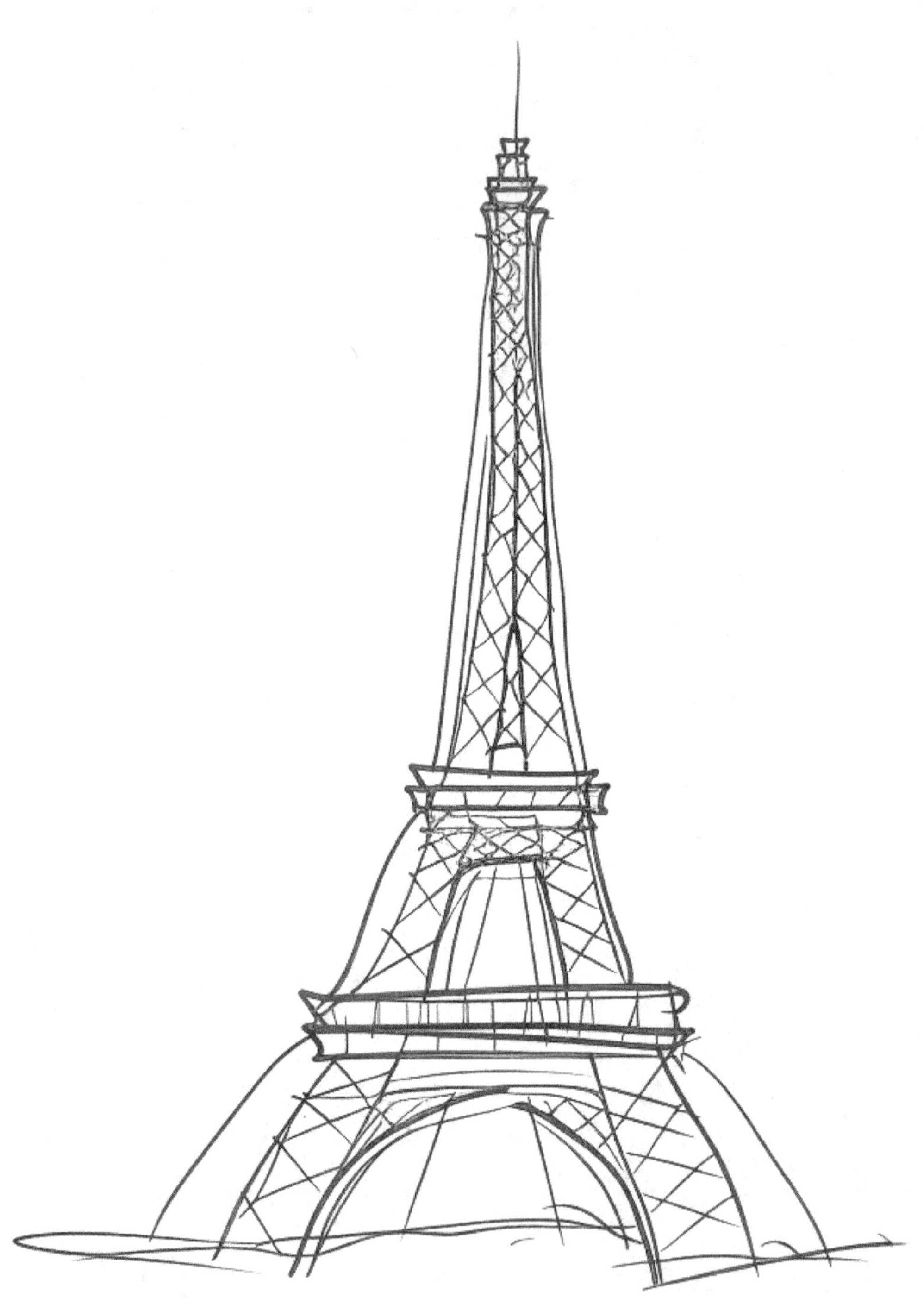

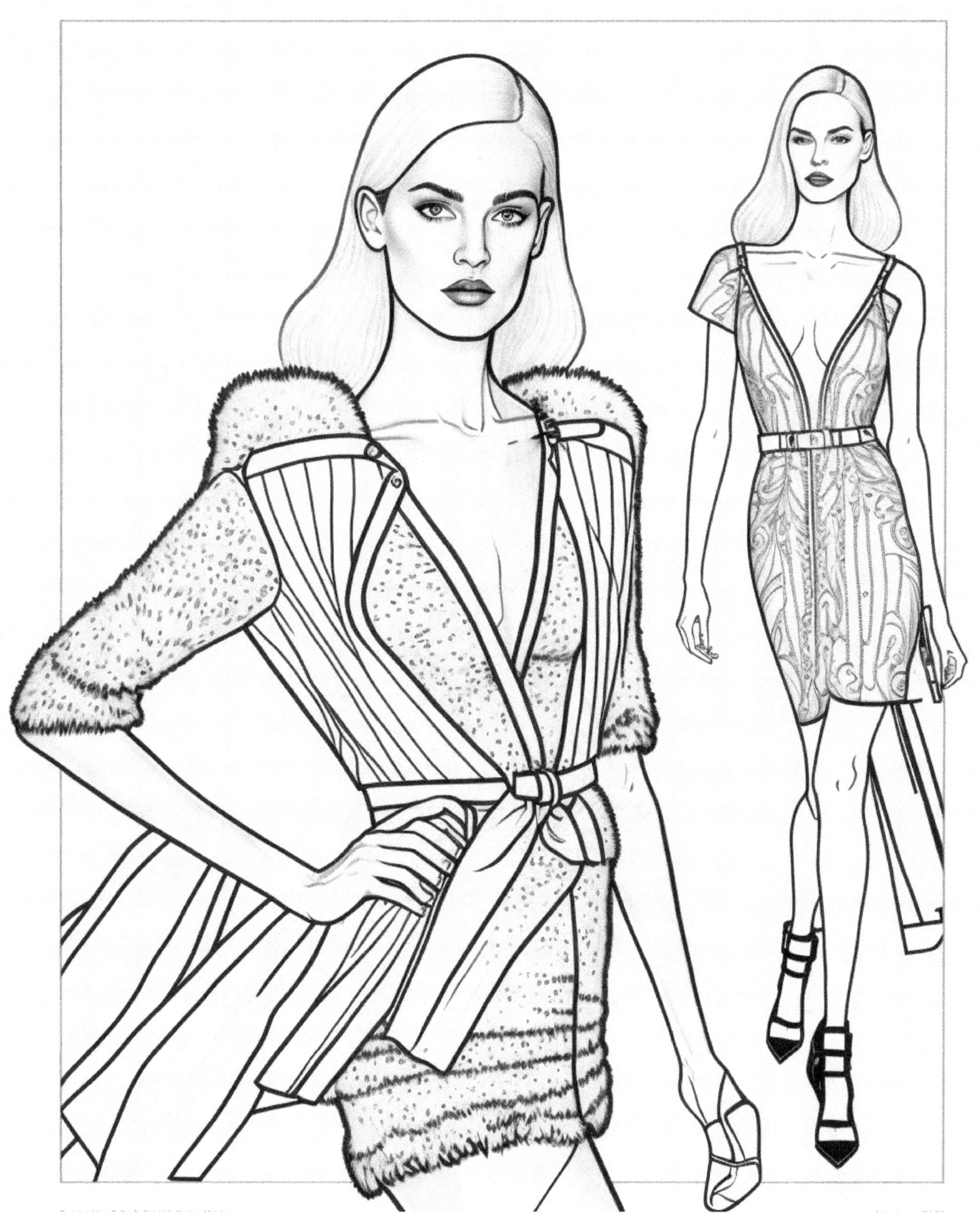

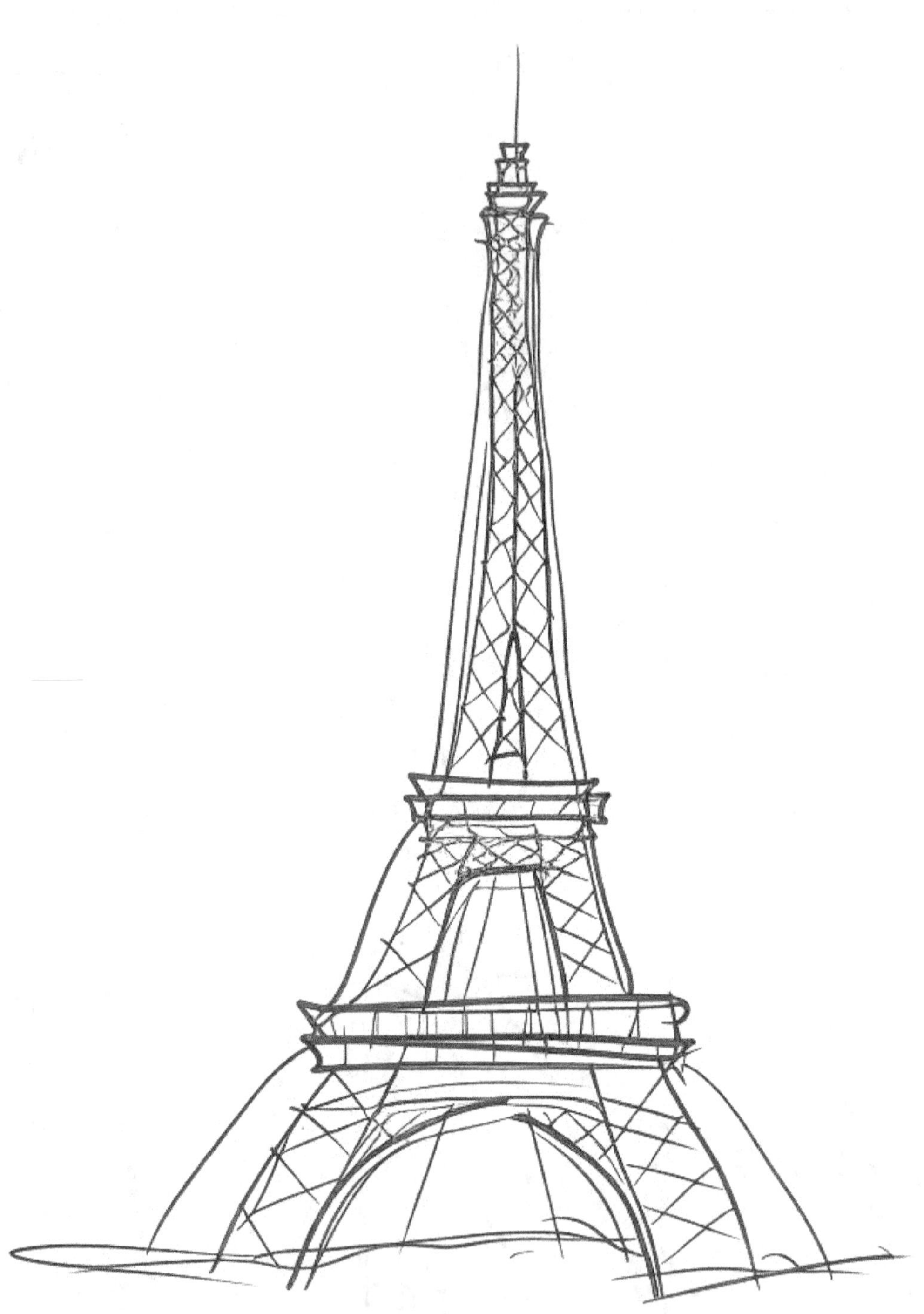

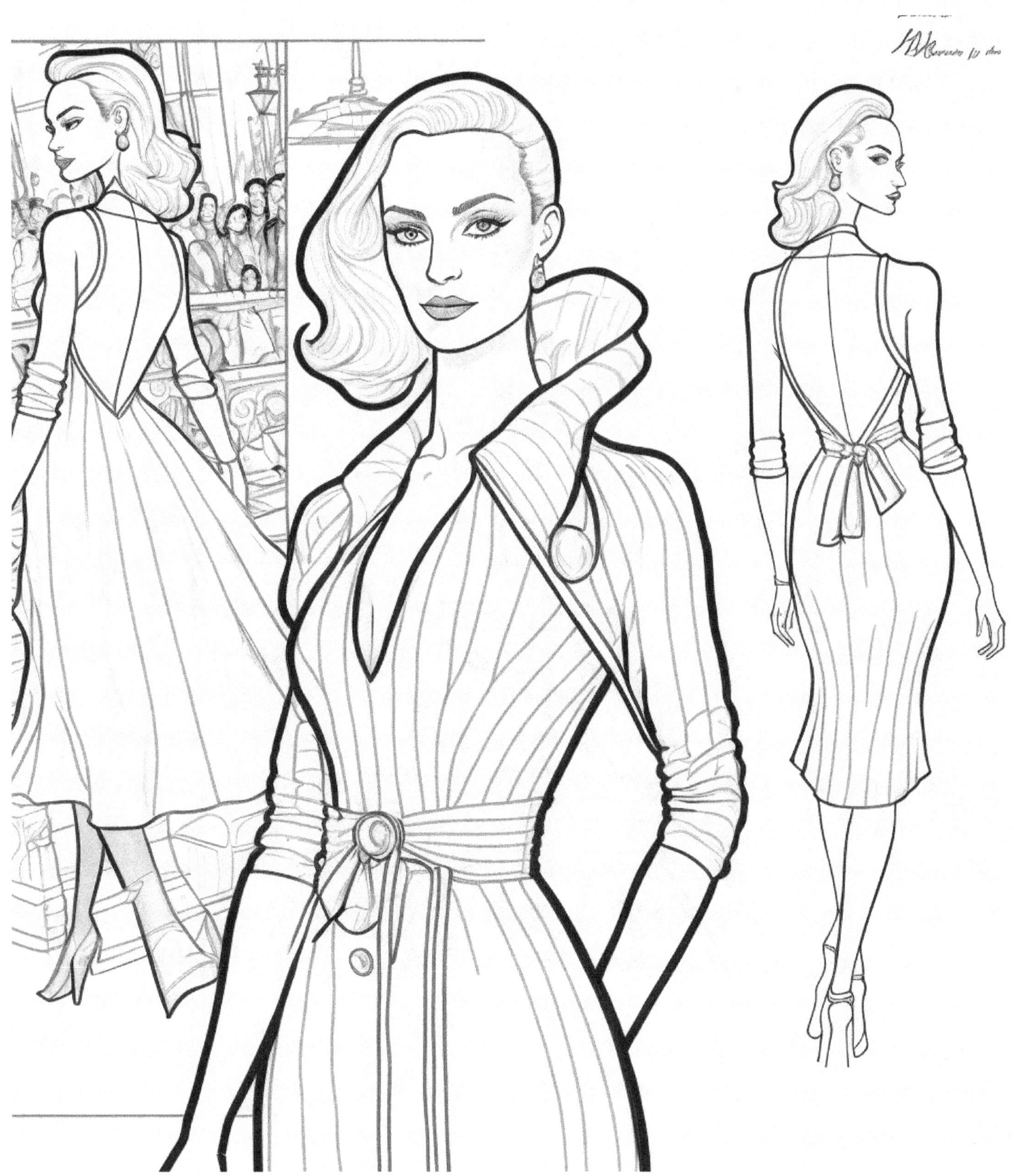

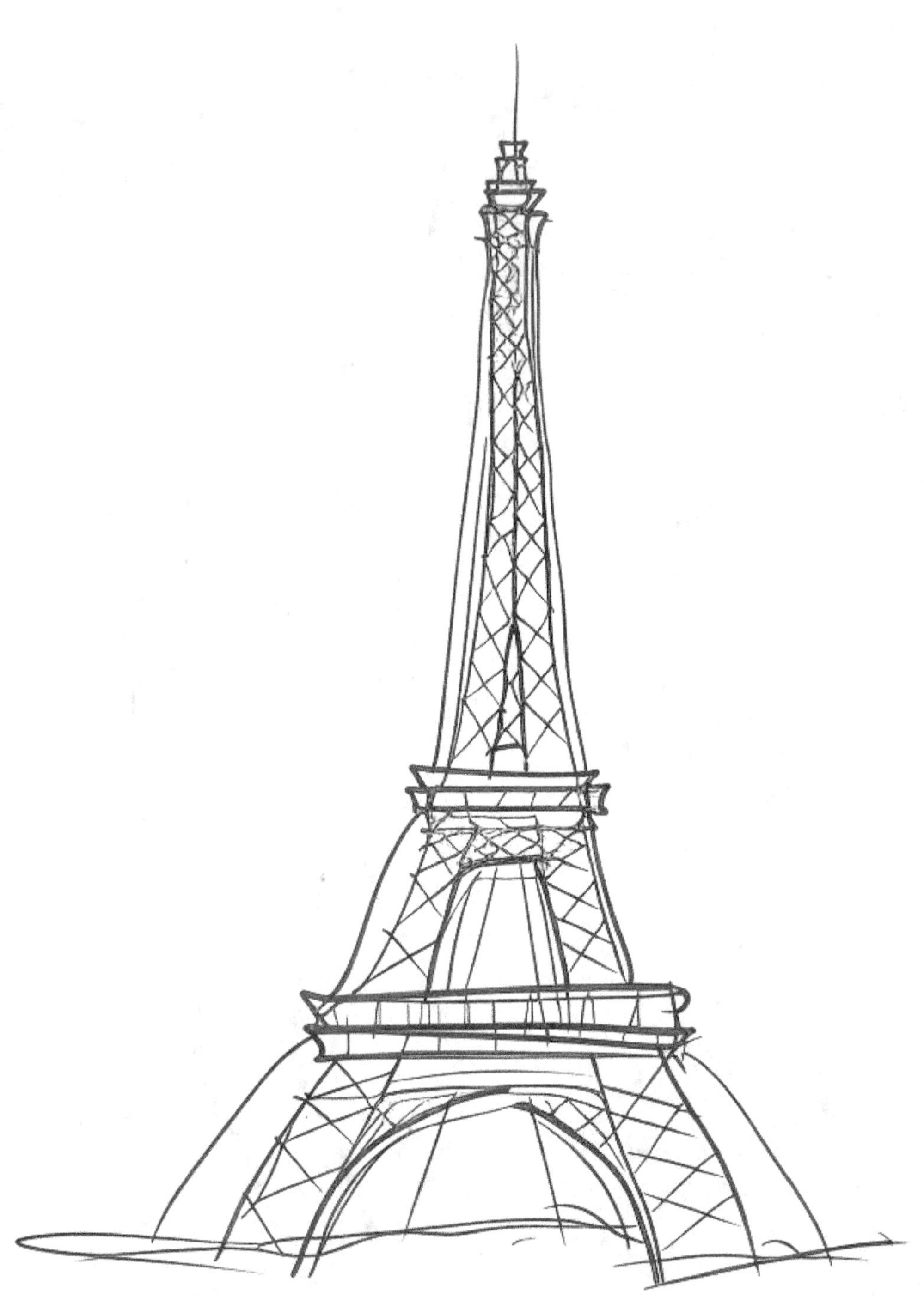

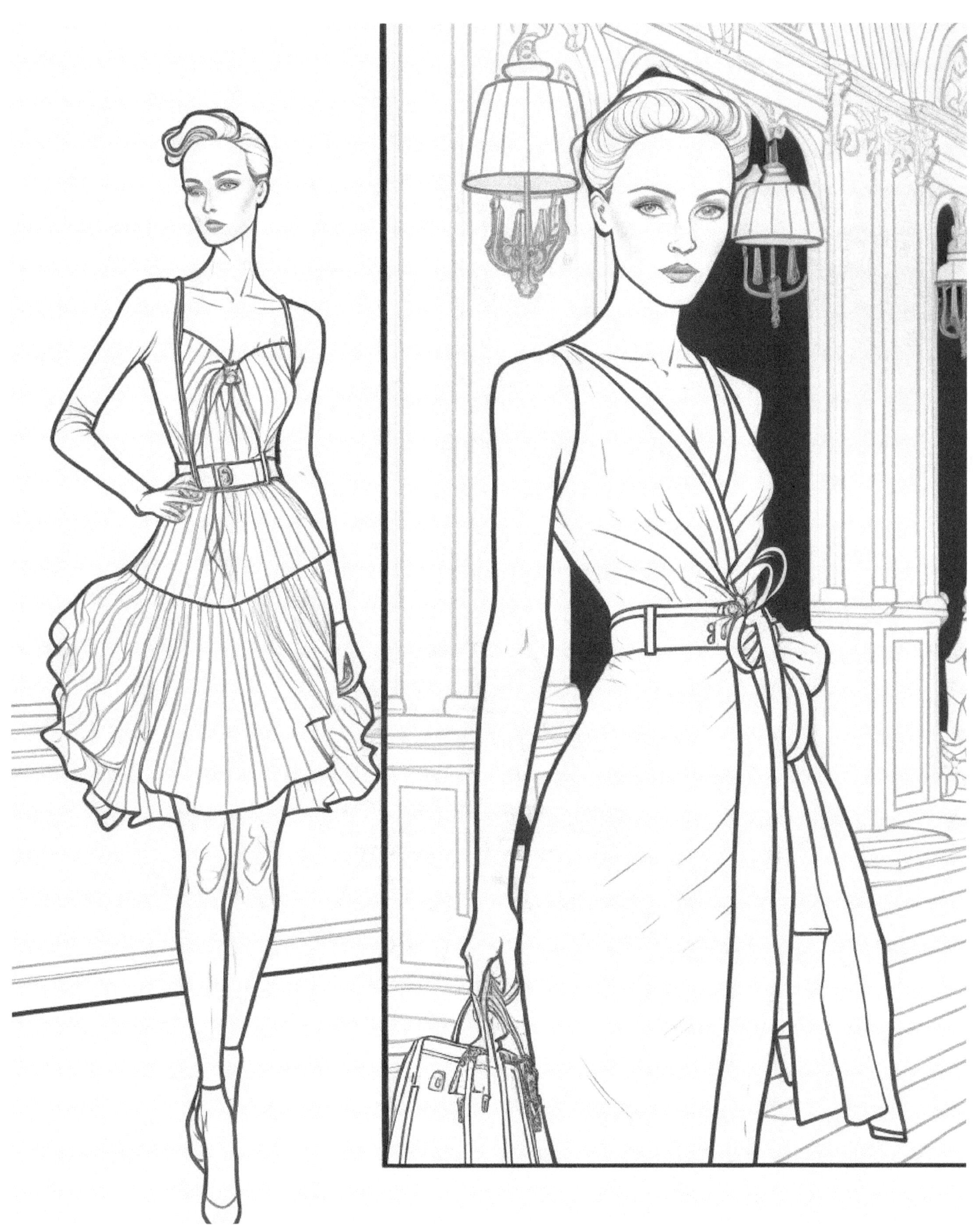

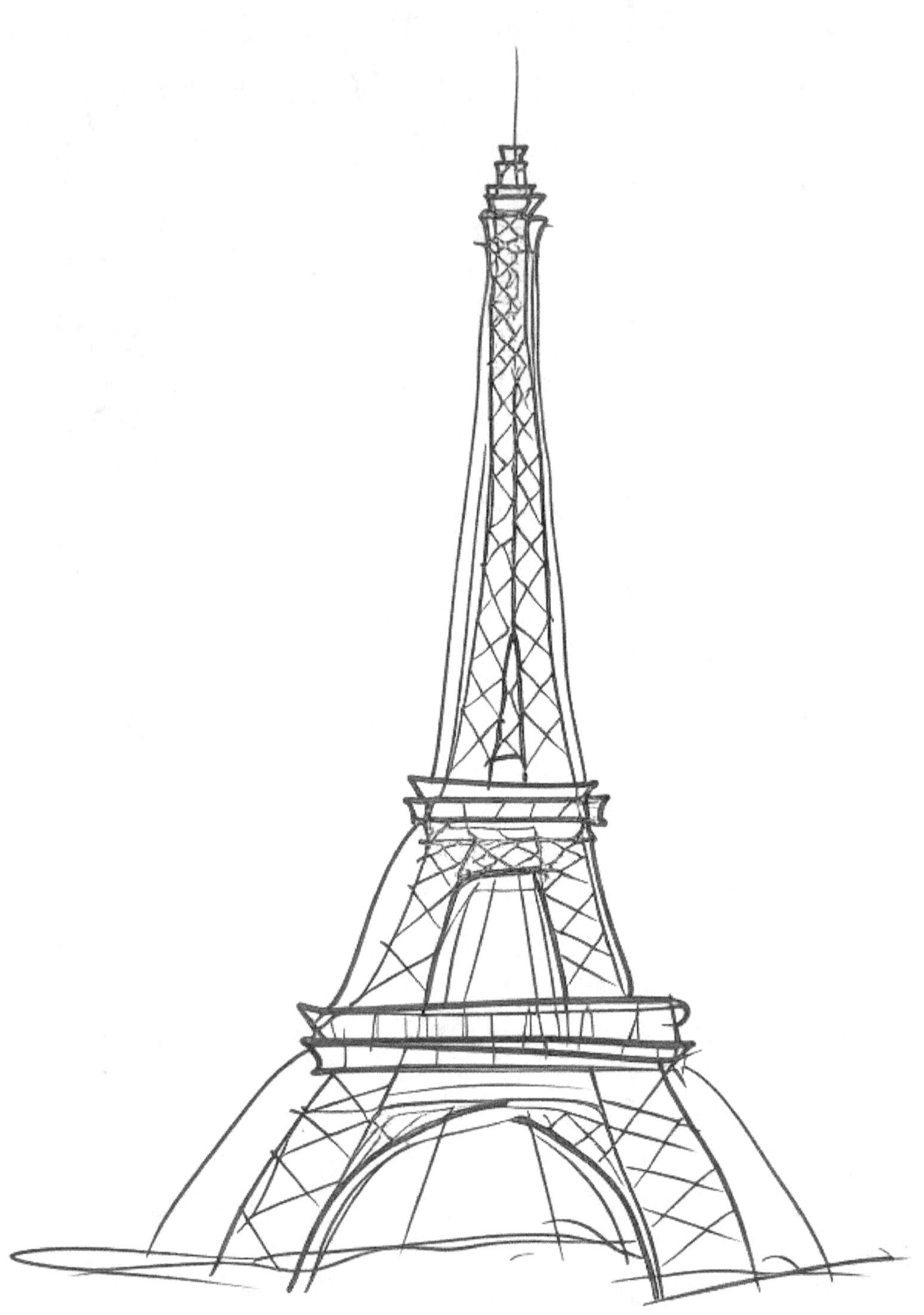

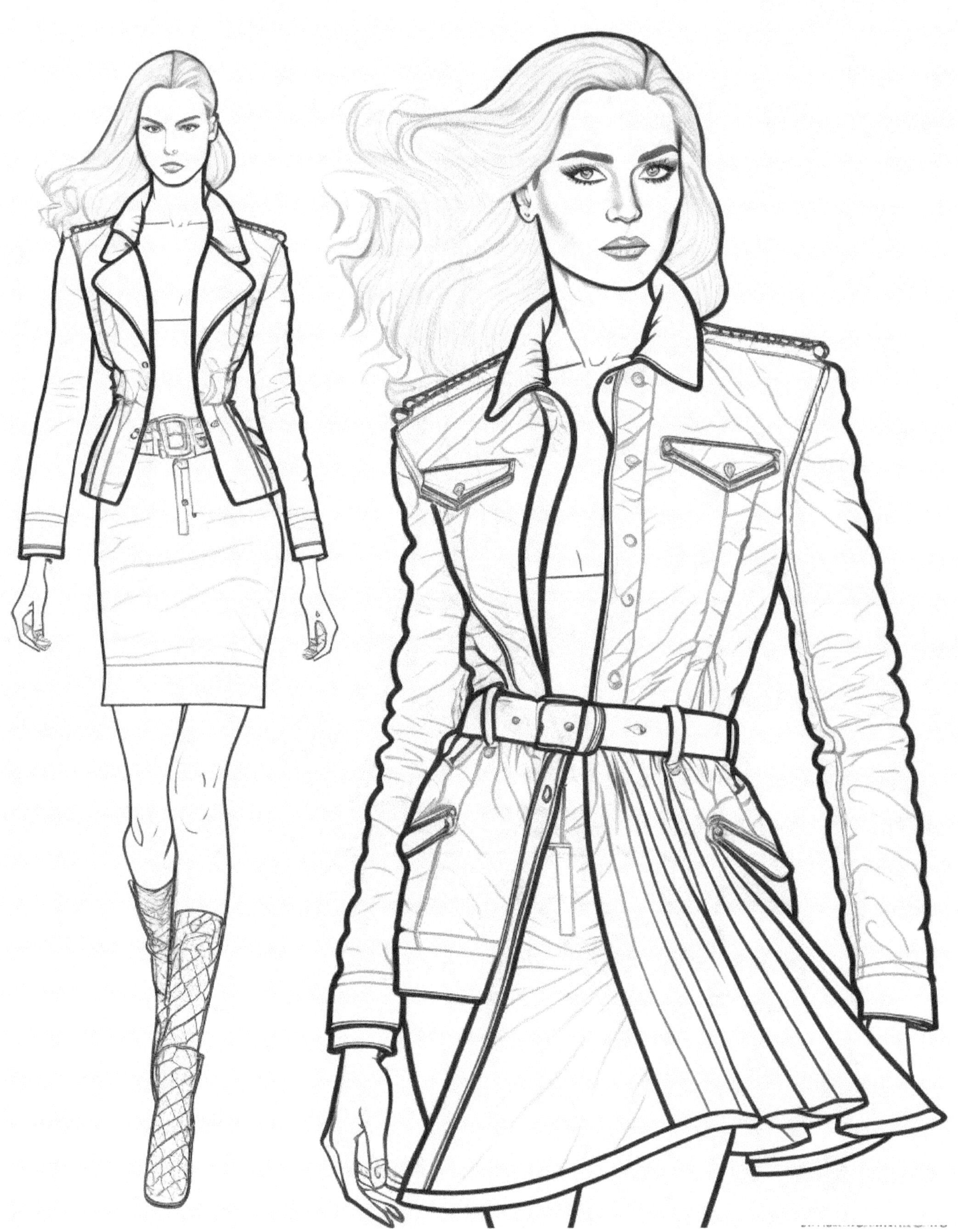

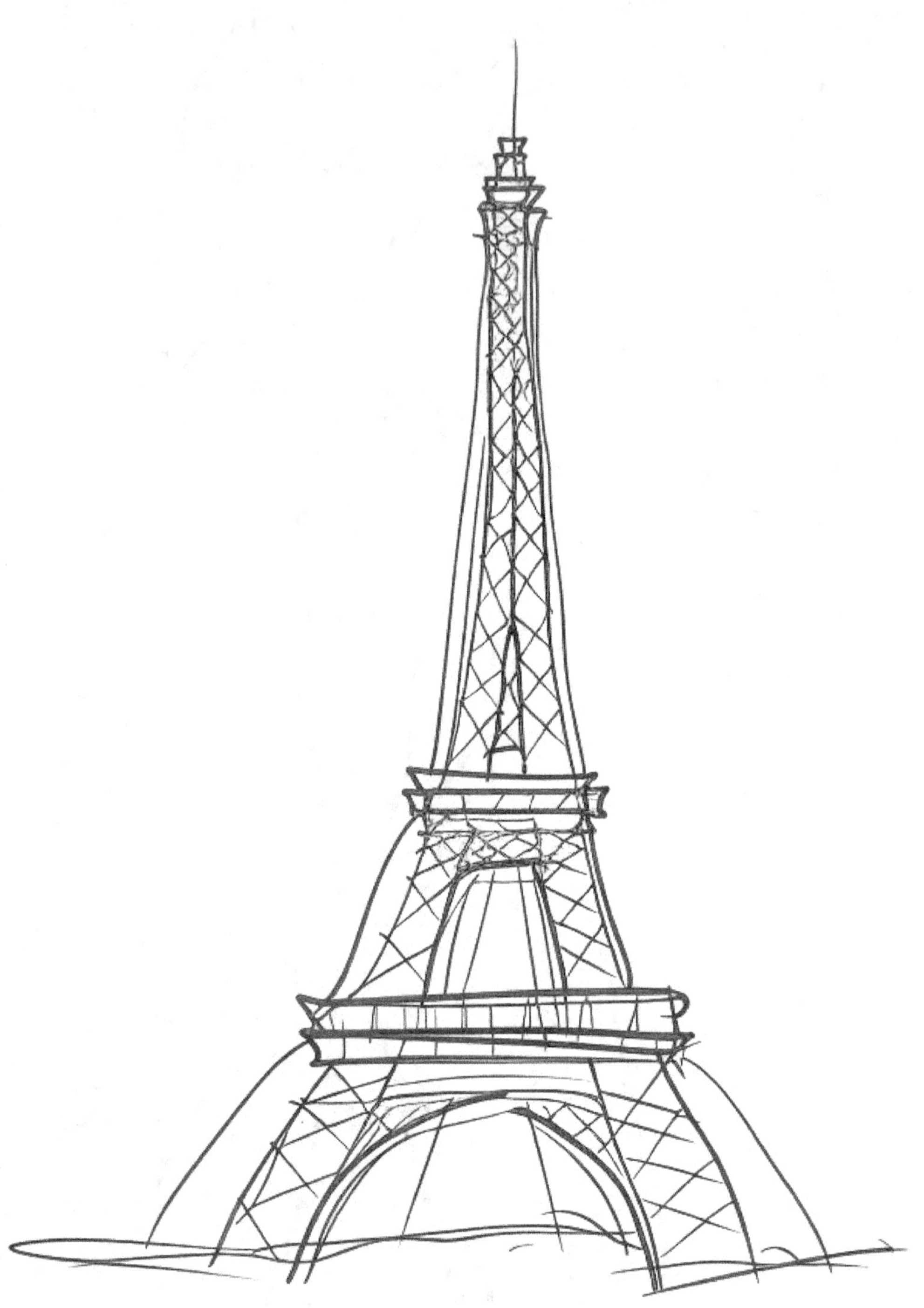

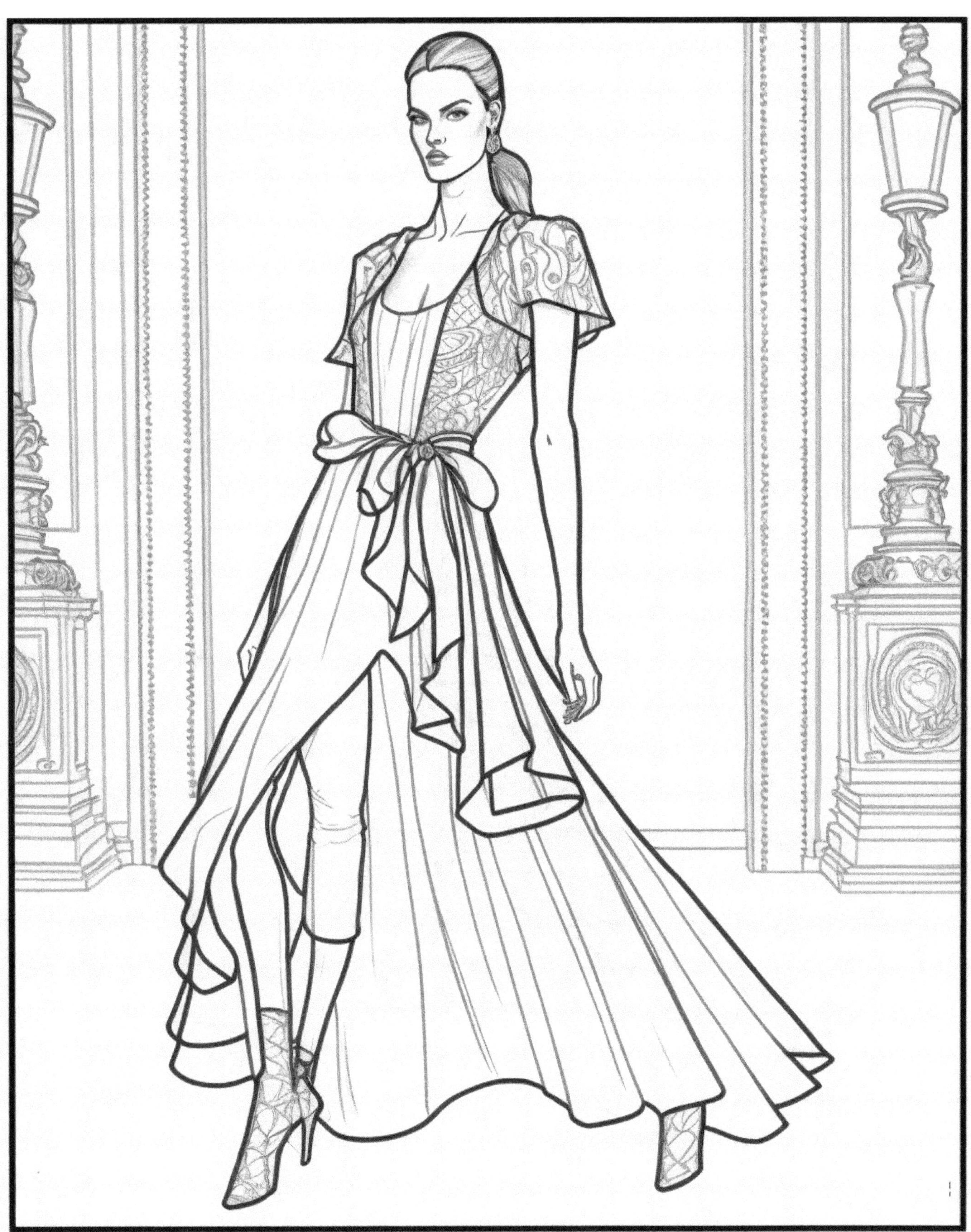

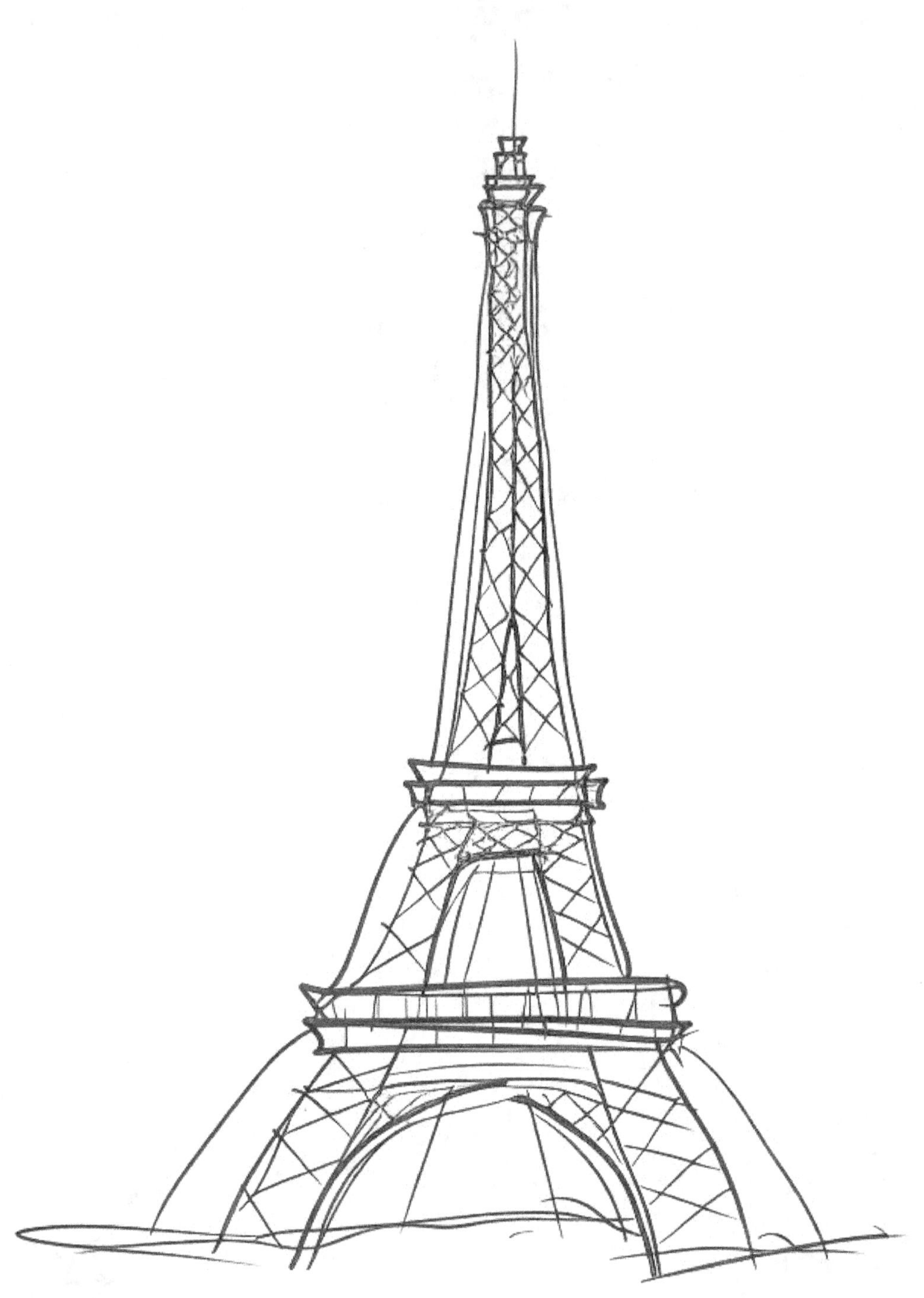

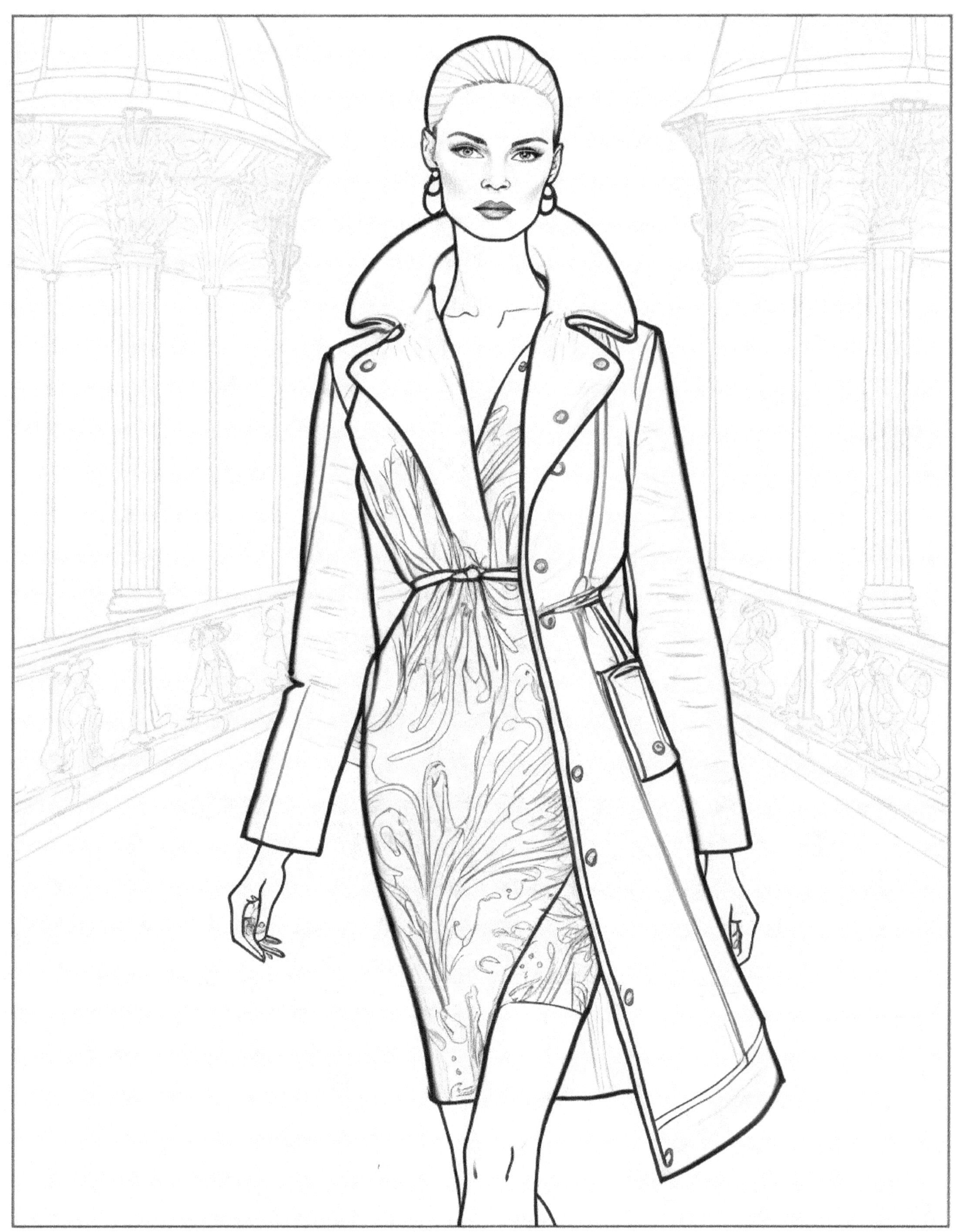

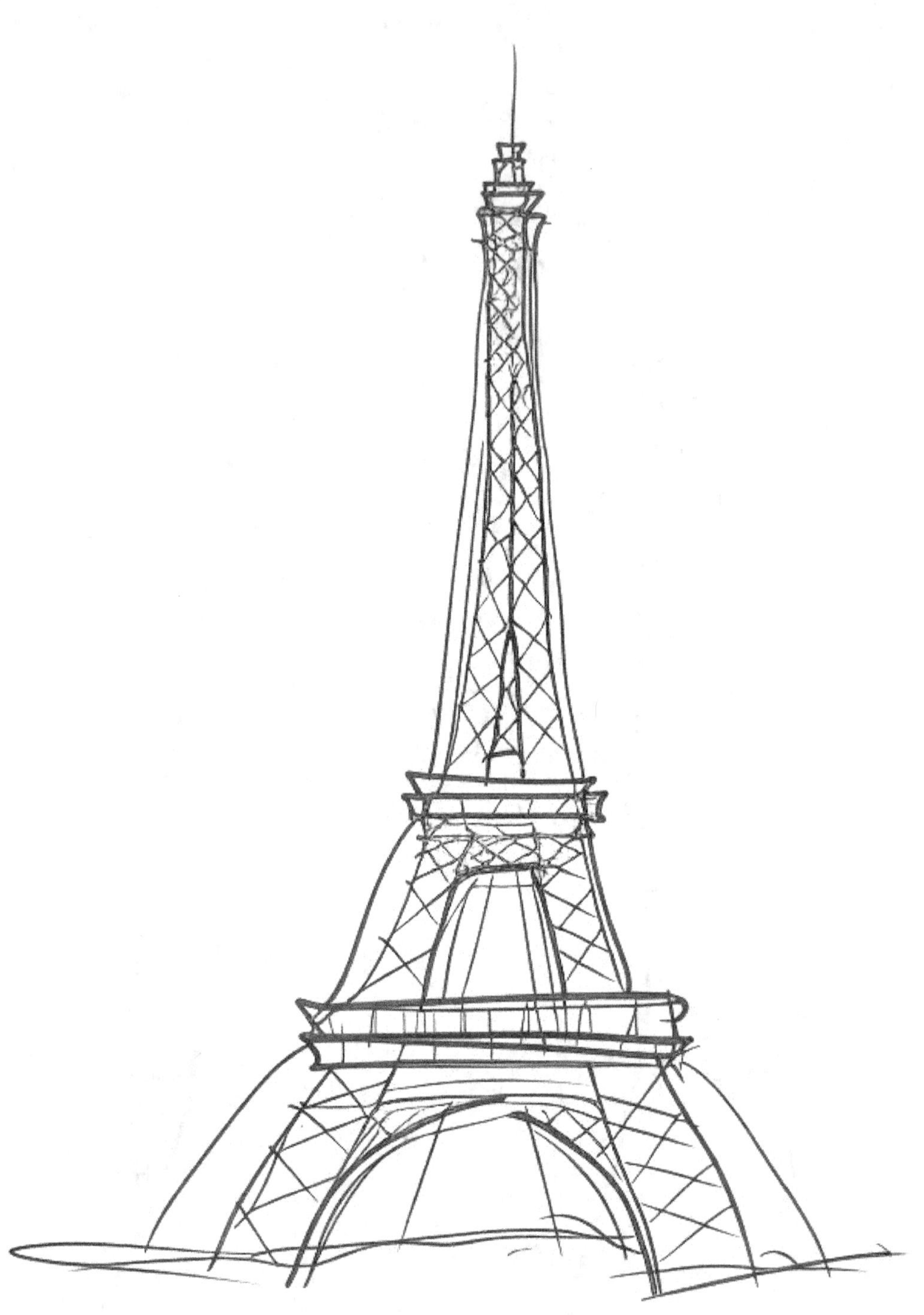

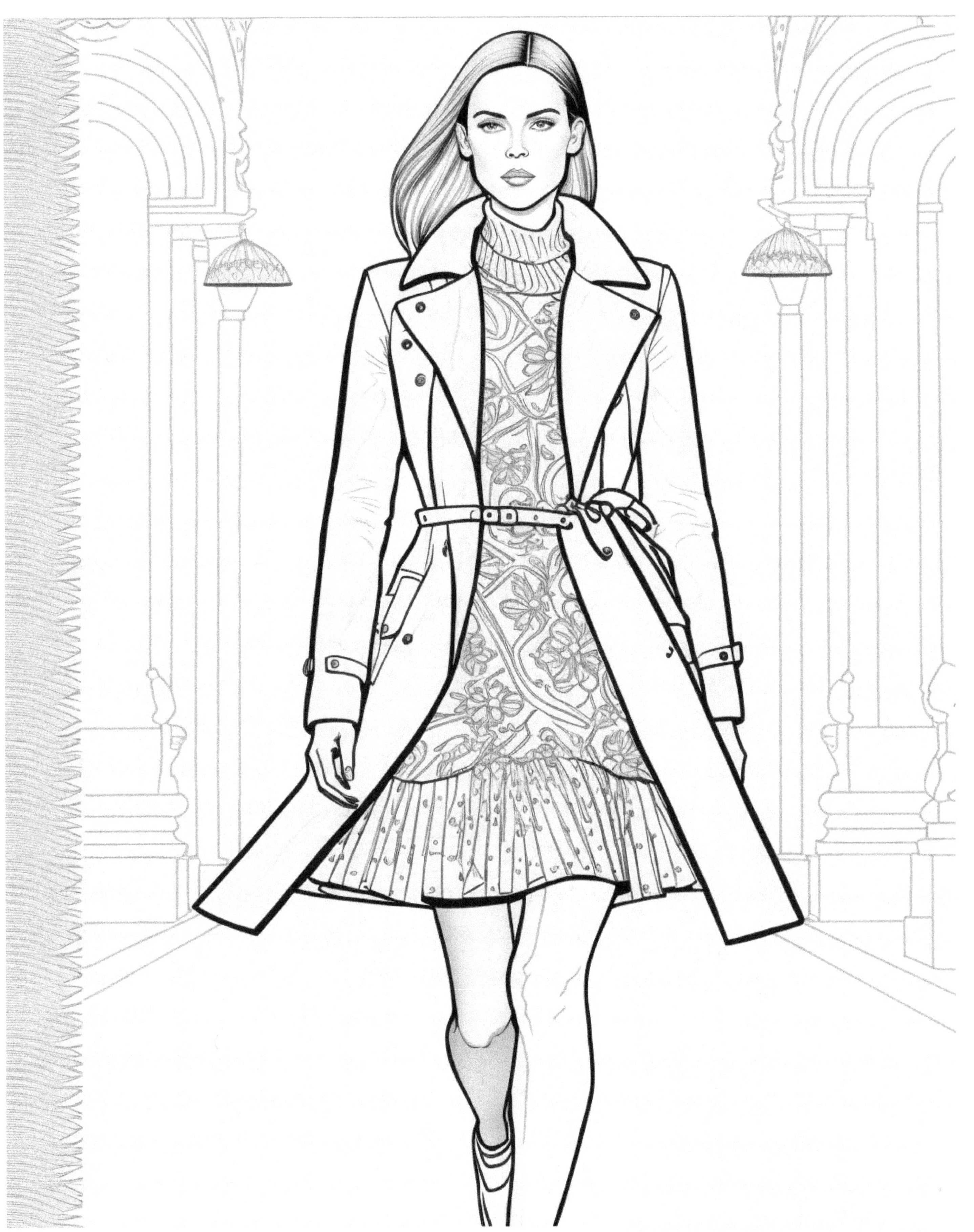

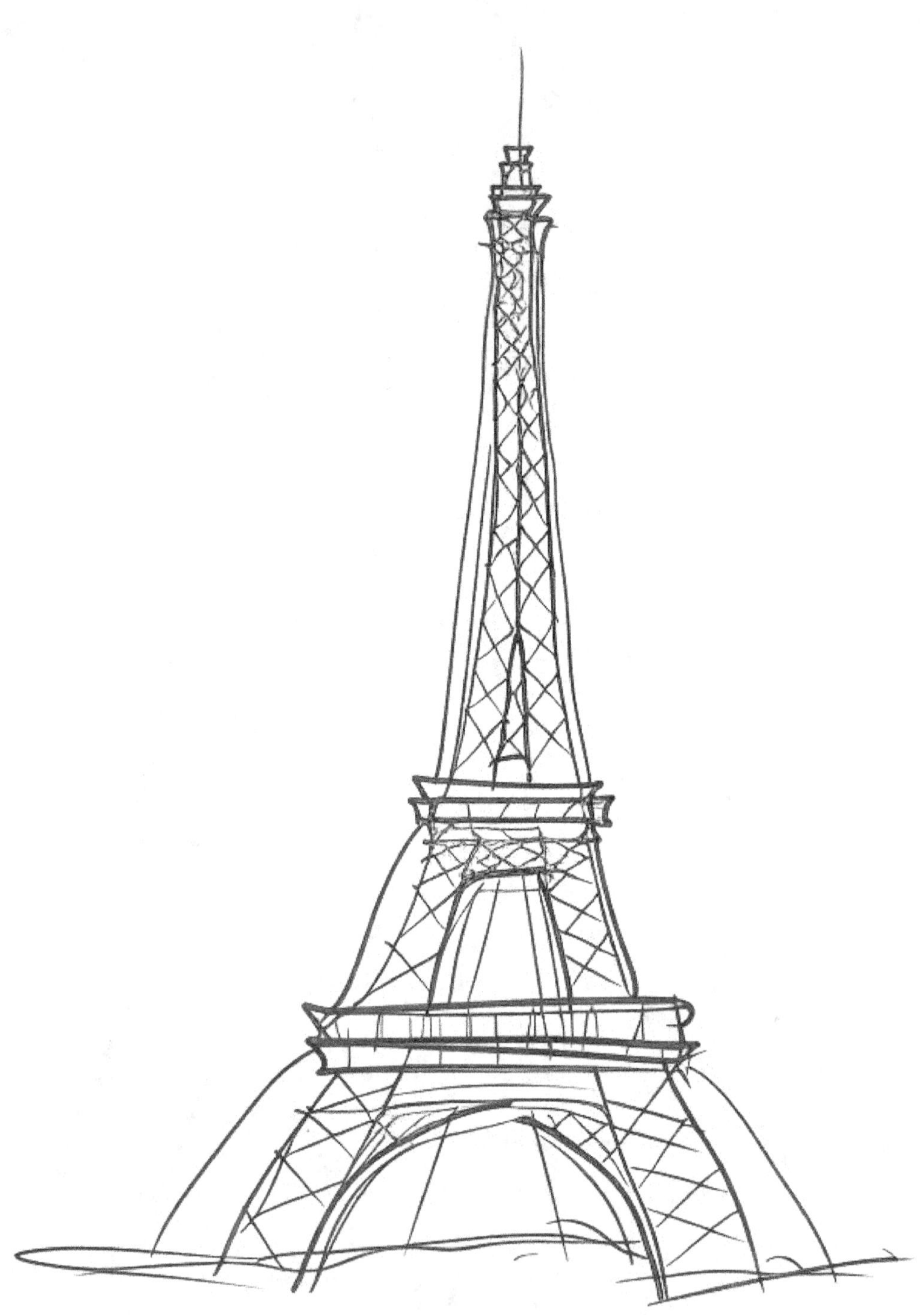

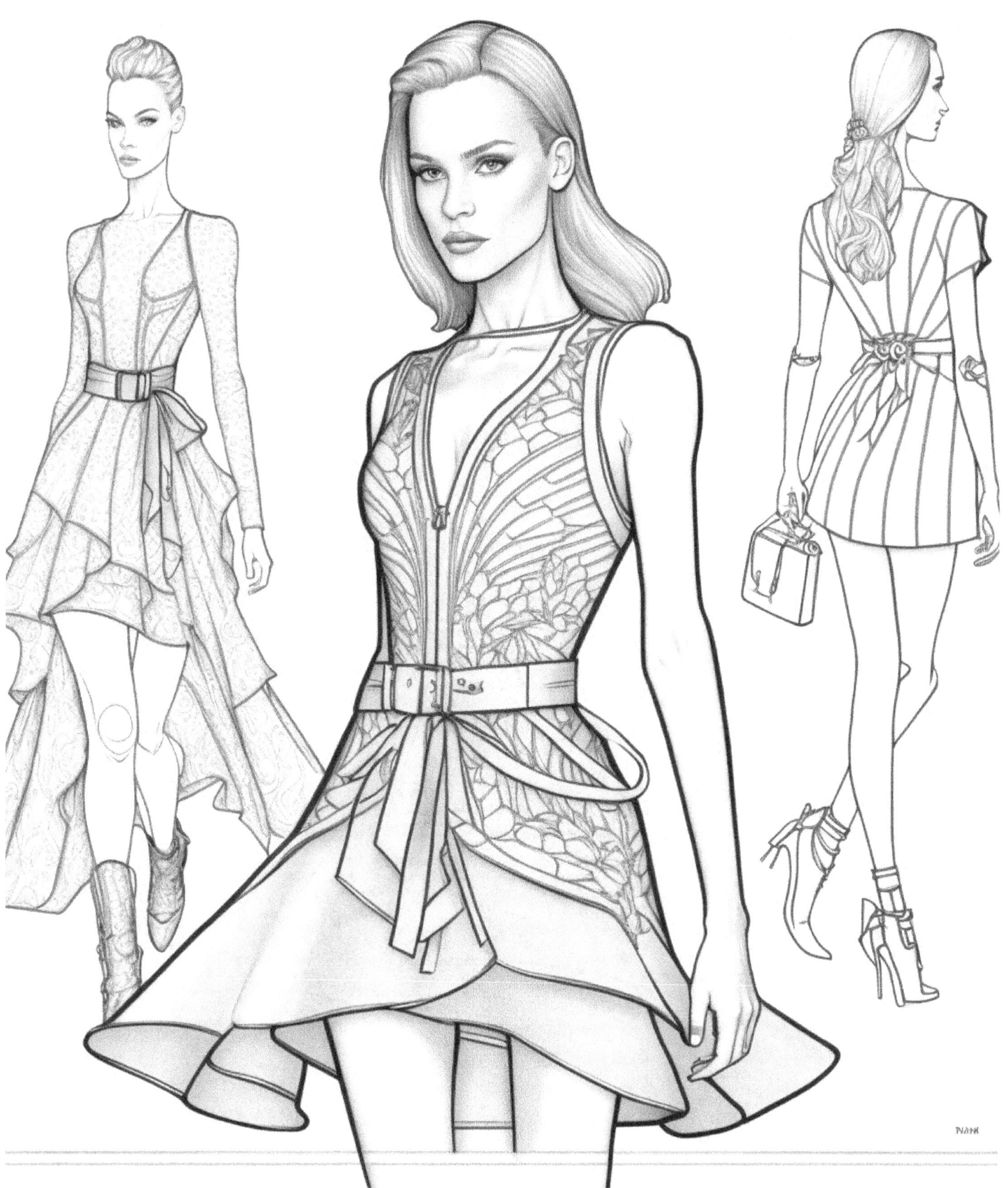

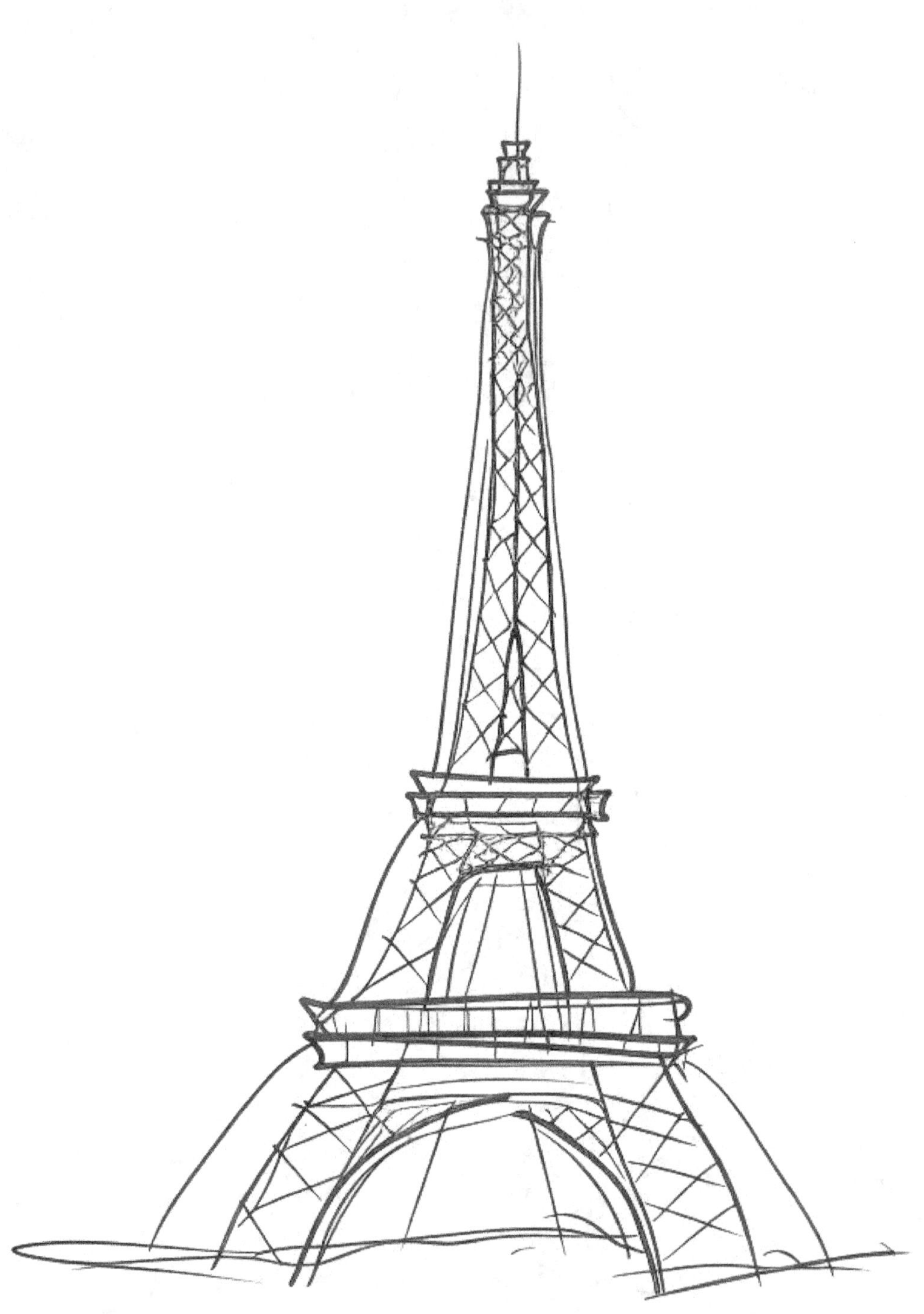

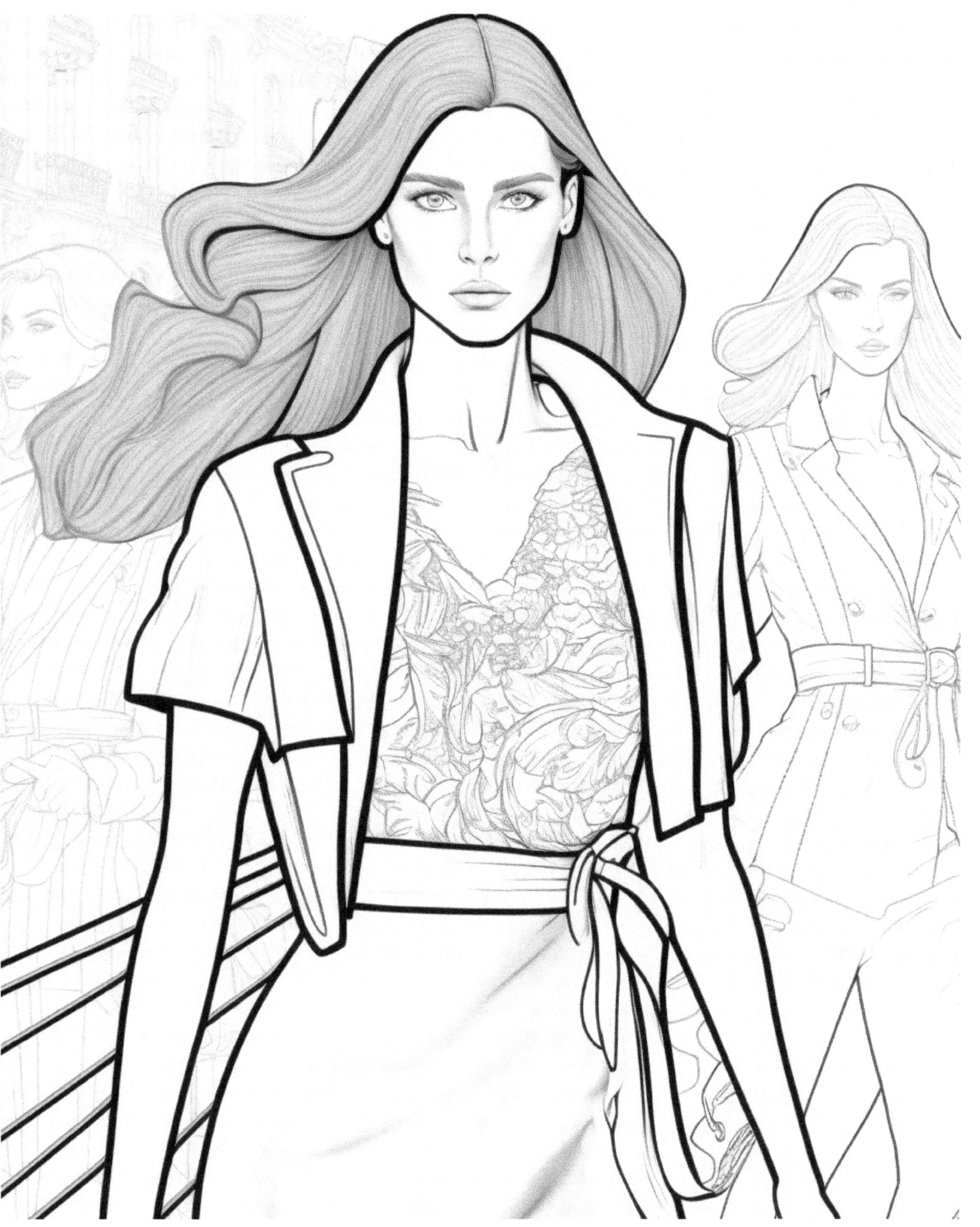